# KEEP MOVING 4WARD

## WHAT IT TAKES TO BE AN ENTREPRENEUR

# BRADLEY LOISELLE

Copyright © 2013 Bradley Loiselle

**Library and Archives Canada Cataloguing in Publication**

Loiselle, Bradley, author
   Keep moving 4ward : what it takes to be an entrepreneur / Bradley Loiselle.

Issued in print and electronic formats.
ISBN 978-0-9919856-0-9 (pbk.).--ISBN 978-0-9919856-1-6 (epub).--
ISBN 978-0-9919856-2-3 (mobi).--ISBN 978-0-9919856-3-0 (pdf)

   1. Entrepreneurship. 2. New business enterprises. 3. Success in business.
I. Title. II. Title: Keep moving forward.

HD62.5.L64 2013          658.1'1          C2013-904612-7
                                          C2013-904613-5


Published by Bradley Loiselle
www.keepmoving4ward.com

"Disney" is a registered trademark owned by Disney Enterprises, Inc.


Models and processes: Bradley Loiselle
Photography: Bradley Loiselle and Michel Loiselle
Inside text design and production: PageWave Graphics Inc.
Illustrations: Crowle Art Group
Copy editors: Lloyd Davis, Jonathan Webb and Bruce Porter
Proofreader: Barbara Kamienski

Printed and bound in China

1  2  3  4  5  TOP  17  16  15  14  13

*This book is dedicated to my family.*

*To my wife, Nathalie, who has supported me unconditionally throughout all my business ventures, both failures and successes.*

*To my children — Eric, Alexandra and Kloé for being my inspiration to keep moving forward.*

*Thank you all so very much! I love you.*

# Contents

# Acknowledgements

In the writing of this book many factors helped shape my way of thinking and the content within these pages, but in the end we are all a sum of our experiences.

First of all, I would like to thank all of my family and friends who supported me over the years, listened to me talk about some of my crazy ideas, some of which actually worked and others not so much, but in the end they were there when I needed help.

Special thanks to my wife, Nathalie, who has been there since day one supporting me and encouraging me.

And to Scott Hunter, my former employer, peer and now business partner: you have been a great balance to my energized, fast-reacting business style. I have enjoyed the many years we have had together and expect many more to come.

And to my employees over my many businesses, thank you for your hard work, your loyalty and dedication to my vision.

And to my business advisors and friends over the many years of meeting with me to discuss strategies, business issues and next steps: Tony Keenan, Bill Kennedy, David Appotive, and my dearly departed Jim Rayburn and Paul Cross. You are very much missed!

To the educational system that did not provide the necessary tools and resources to support entrepreneurs like me: I want to thank you for making me who I am today by forcing me to learn and experience entrepreneurship the hard way.

# Preface

*Keep Moving 4ward* is a book that dives into the world of a struggling dreamer who made his dreams come true without having to sacrifice everything along the way.

My dreams started from the inside of a dumpster bin, where I spent many weekends hoping to find a child's playground in a pile of garbage. This book will tell how, from that rough beginning, someone with no formal education, no money and no industry experience could, in a very short time, become the founder of Canada's largest supplier of licensed paper goods, partnering with every major entertainment company in North America. Success came to me through determination and persistence; it was built with what I call "the power of leverage."

As you move through the book, you will experience my struggles and come to understand the steps I took to change my life and, in the process, build two successful businesses. Through my life experiences, my illustrations and my ideas, I will help you understand the techniques I used to achieve my goals. My ideas are not new, but I explain them in a way I hope will make them easy to understand. I offer real-life experiences instead of traditional theories. I hope you find them entertaining, engaging and educational.

If you are one of those people who fear they will never amount to anything, this book tells you that you may not be able to choose how you start your life, but you *can* choose whether it becomes a success. I believe success will come to those who believe in themselves no matter their situation, their education or what other people might tell them. If you have a dream, never give up. Believe, achieve and you will succeed. Keep moving forward!

# Icons Used in This Book

Being an entrepreneur means looking for the simplest path to understanding a lesson in order to get quick results. I have included a series of icons that will help point out when there is something I think you should take note of.

 **Traits that make a good entrepreneur.** Knowing whether you have the traits typical of an entrepreneur will help you determine if you should go into business for yourself or not.

 **Pitfalls you should be aware of when you are building your business.** There are many things that can go wrong and influences that can take you down the wrong path. These are perils you need to steer clear of.

 **Personal experiences that provide an example of a lesson being put into action.** These will help you see the relevance of a particular point and how it might be used in your own development.

 **Critical elements that are an absolute must in building a business.**

# Introduction

HAVE YOU EVER WONDERED HOW SOME PEOPLE are able to achieve the impossible? We've all dreamt about being rich and famous, but what makes a dream become a reality? The answer is much simpler than you might think: you. When you take action—planning and using the right tools and resources—anything can happen. Some dreamers only dream, but there are those of us who make the decision to make our dreams come true. We are called entrepreneurs.

In early 2010 I heard a speech by one of the directors of the local Entrepreneur Centre that really made me think more about what it means to be an entrepreneur. He cited a recent study on the career goals of school-aged children. The study revealed that 40 per cent of children aspire to go into business for themselves when they grow up. That number astonished me, but what he said next was even more surprising: there are no real programs in our education system to instruct and support this large number of aspiring entrepreneurs. Because of this, I would assume that the majority of these children never get the opportunity to realize their dreams.

Think of a world without entrepreneurs: we would not have developed the telephone, the automobile, the refrigerator, the toothbrush, the light bulb, the computer, the modern house—the list goes on. Our society, as it exists today, has been built on the innovation and creativity of entrepreneurship. So many things we use started out as ideas developed by someone with enough courage to take action. We all have great ideas, and my hope with this book is to help you move closer to developing your ideas and creating your own success.

One of the biggest constraints holding people back from starting their own business is fear: fear of financial instability, fear of embarrassment, fear of the unknown and fear of failure. There are more financial self-help books on the market than I'm able to count, but they mostly focus on long-term goals through safe investment and saving money. Saving is important to ensuring a comfortable retirement and a secure financial future, but in my opinion, for what you might gain tomorrow, you will lose today.

Life is short and full of the unexpected. Focusing only on retirement will cost you in opportunities today. "Opportunity cost" occurs when you give up one thing at the expense of something else. When you don't take that vacation or cooking class because you're always putting your money aside, you're losing out on the things you could be doing today. Saving is important, but so is living in the now. Most people fall into the trap of only living their lives from day to day. They have bills to pay, responsibilities to keep and families to support, and they never really look beyond those responsibilities—they want to, but they're afraid they can't. These are important aspects of life that need to be considered before moving into a career as an entrepreneur.

So how do you get what you want today without sacrificing your dreams? One of the aims of this book, based on my own life and business experiences, is to give you my answer to this challenge.

• • • • •

When I was young, what I wanted more than anything was to grow up, have a family and be able to provide them with the opportunities I never had. This is the story of how I dreamt about becoming greater than I was, and then did it. It's about making things happen, teaching the dreamer in all of us how to turn away the naysayers and pessimists and, through hard work and perseverance, turn our dreams into realities.

I had everything working against me growing up, but I didn't let that stop me. It wasn't easy, but after years of hard work, part-time jobs and many failed business attempts, I finally built my own multimillion-dollar company, one of the fastest-growing partners to the Walt Disney company. I stayed in business for close to a decade and drew a six-figure salary (although, for many years before that, I worked without drawing any salary at all). Unfortunately, because of the recession and other factors, I had to close that business. Closing it did not make the venture any less successful; I learned from my experience and started over. As I was writing this book, I was the founder and president of another fast-growing company, iPal Interactive Learning. Only 18 months after I launched it, I sold it in a very financially and professionally advantageous deal. What the successful building and sale of iPal tells me is that I had learned from my mistakes and had done it right this time, that I do indeed have the right approach and sound business sense. I know how to be smart in applying the lessons experience has taught me. Today, my successes far outnumber my failures. If I can do it, anyone can.

The successes didn't happen through magic, though. I can attribute most of what I have achieved to what I like to call the "power of leverage," an idea I developed that became the foundation on which I built my business and continue to build my success. It is a technique to use when you have to get what you need in order to achieve your goals. It took me years of experience to figure it out, but after being knocked down and bouncing back up so many times, I am finally ready to pass on my knowledge to others.

This book tells the story of how I grew from a dumpster-diving, introverted teenager with no formal post-secondary education into the builder and owner of a multimillion-dollar company. It also gives a lot of information and advice on how to plan, develop and sell a business. The book is neither an autobiography as such, nor a strictly business-planning book, but it combines many elements of both. I am using the story of my own life and business experiences to pass on the lessons I have learned to new entrepreneurs and would-be entrepreneurs. The business advice I give is hardly new, but my hope is that, presented in the context of an actual living example—my own life and business story—it may be of some practical use and inspiration to others.

# The Dumpster Diving Years

1

WE DIDN'T HAVE MUCH WHEN I WAS GROWING up. Most of the time, going to school, all we had was a sandwich, which consisted 95 percent of the time of mock chicken, which is the reason I never eat that concoction today. I rarely had drinks or treats and was always hungry. My mom often left notes in my lunch box telling me how proud she was of me, and that helped to ease the grumbling in my stomach. After school, when I returned home, to ensure that I was not going to eat more than my share, I was forbidden from opening the fridge without permission, but I did get a snack. This consisted of crackers with Cheez Whiz or toast with mustard, salt and pepper. I used to joke that this was a poor boy's pizza, because if you really imagined it was pizza, it kind of tasted like one, or so I told myself.

My mother never really worked when we were children, only because she wanted to make sure she was there for us. Her heart was definitely in the right place; however, the environment we were in sometimes made me question her decision. She had been through a tough situation with my biological father, and this was why she was so protective of my brothers and me. The unfortunate part was that our stepfather was not the best role model. I used to wonder why the government would give a family of six so little money for food. When I got older, I realized that it wasn't that they gave us too little, but rather that the money was mismanaged. I later recalled that, on the first day of each month after we received our government cheque, my stepfather would spend half the day travelling on the bus to a store in Hull, Quebec, to pick up six to eight cans of tobacco because it was cheaper than purchasing it in Ottawa. He would then return home and pack the cans in our freezer so the tobacco would stay fresh longer. As a result, there was little space left in the freezer, or much money left for food.

There wasn't much to do in our neighbourhood, which I think sparked my **creativity**, as I was left alone with my imagination quite frequently. I think this is also when I learned how to draw. I would spend hours doodling cartoon characters and setting the stage for their adventures.

Think outside the box

My clothes were almost always hand-me-downs, articles that, for the most part, had been purchased secondhand. They were worn and ripped sometimes, and definitely not in style. I didn't mind them so much, aside from how they fit. My shoes were so tight that my feet hurt and over time grew curved. My second-largest toe on each foot took the shape of the curve of the shoe, inward like a hammer claw. When I was older, my doctor told me my feet had not been allowed the room they needed to grow properly in my ill-fitting shoes. For decades, I was embarrassed about my feet and envious of family members and friends who were able to wear sandals and walk barefoot without being self-conscious, as I was. I eventually came to realize, when I was 39, that my worries about my feet were minor in comparison to the real problems we have in society, and that was when I bought my first pair of open-toed sandals.

## We all have insecurities! Putting them in perspective to life around us will make us realize what is important and what is not

One day when I was 13, my brothers and I were wandering aimlessly around our neighbourhood looking for something to do when we came across some dumpsters behind a local shopping mall. I don't recall the first time I crawled inside the garbage bins, but I clearly remember how excited I was when I began opening up the bags and boxes to see what we could find. It made me nervous to be in there; I was afraid we would get caught, or even worse, that the bin would be picked up by the garbage truck and we'd be crushed alive. But all it took was finding one toy among all that trash and I was hooked. I told no one about my little "shopping sprees," but I did them all the time with the passion of an explorer. It's incredible to think what people will do when they have so little. What I most enjoyed about garbage picking was the anticipation of what I might find. It was like opening presents daily. Tearing away the box lids or ripping into the plastic garbage bags felt great. You were sure that the next bag could be the one—the one that held all the treasures.

We didn't have much at any time when I was a child, but it was on special occasions that all the things we went without hit home. Most of our Christmas and birthday gifts were clothes, and there is nothing wrong with clothes, but we all know what it's like as a child to open a present and realize it is just a pair of socks. Children want toys, but toys are expensive. One of the best Christmases I can remember was when I was 13. On Christmas Eve, we went through the garbage bin, as we had done so many times before, behind Consumers Distributing at Westgate Shopping Centre. Usually, when you jump into a dumpster, your landing is cushioned by the bags and papers inside. When I jumped in that day, bruising my tailbone with the hard, abrupt landing, I knew something was different. As I sifted through the layers of stuff, I realized that the bin was filled with toys. They were broken toys, of course, but I didn't care. We took them home and spent the day trying to fix them. It was a great day. I felt I had the greatest gift ever.

When it came to birthdays, I was luckier than my brothers, because mine fell on the last day of the month. That was when the government cheque was picked up, and that meant there was more money in the house than at any other time of the month. My mom would sometimes give me a little extra that day, and she was so proud to be able to do it. On this day, my mom was very much like her mother, who was always trying to find ways to spoil us. My grandmother also stayed close to us—she lived in the same building, only eight floors down. My brothers and I loved going to see her because her world was all about making us happy when we were there. Her house was always immaculate, with furniture that was free from dust and smelled like lemons. She always made sure her home was ready for guests. She didn't have much company aside from my family, and she always made us feel welcome, hugging us tightly while patting our backs rapidly. She always dressed as if she was heading out on the town for tea. Prim and proper she was, words that could never have been used to describe our home upstairs from hers.

My family may have been what most would call dysfunctional, with a stepfather who seemed to care only about himself and a mother who felt trapped in a situation of fear and uncertainty, but today is a much different story. There is much love shared among my brothers, my mother and our kids now. I have a great relationship with my brothers and mother. My children are always excited to see my family when they come over. The bond between my brothers and me is stronger than most because of the hardships we faced together. We would do anything to support one another then and now.

• • • • •

School was not easy for me, and my grades were never great. By the time I was eight, I was already in remedial classes, where I was told by my teacher that I shouldn't set my expectations too high. Both the school and my parents thought there might be something mentally wrong with me. After a while, I began to believe it myself.

When I was 12, my parents decided to have me tested. I remember showing up at the Royal Ottawa Mental Health Centre and being afraid of what they might say and nervous about what they were going to do to me. They took me to a small room, where a doctor attached wires to my hand and head. The room was about 10 feet by 10, with a window looking in from another room where my parents and the doctor looked on. There was a cafeteria-style table and a single chair in the middle of the room. Wires ran up the front of the table to connect into a square device that had more wires sticking out of it, which were later connected to me. No one told me what was happening. All I could think about was Jack Nicholson's character in the film *One Flew Over the Cuckoo's Nest.* "Are they going to electrocute me?" I asked. Of course, they didn't. I was never told the results of the test, but it didn't matter. The experience made me believe there must be something wrong with me.

Things got worse in high school. In my first year, I failed all but one subject. At the end of the school year, I was called into a meeting with my homeroom teacher, guidance counsellor and principal. They were debating what to do with me. All I could think was, "I've failed. I'm a failure." The counsellor told me they had an idea, a way to keep me in the same class as my friends. They had a new program they were testing in our school, for people with reading disorders, and they wanted me to be the first student to try it out. The principal told me they had a feeling that all I needed was help with reading. No one ever told me what the problem was, and to this day I am not sure either, but after learning a bit about dyslexia and attention deficit hyperactivity disorder

(ADHD), I would guess that I probably fit in somewhere on that spectrum. The principal seemed to think that once the reading difficulties were taken care of, the other problems would go away too. He wanted to know if I was willing to give the program a try. I knew I had to do whatever I could at this point. I didn't want to be left behind so, even though I would have to spend an entire semester attending a special class during my lunch period, I agreed to do it.

On the first day of the new school year, I met Mr. Kurnes, the man who would be helping me with my reading skills. The first thing I had to do, he explained, was take some tests to gauge what my reading level was. I started to become very anxious. I remembered the tests I had taken at the Royal Ottawa, with their wires and bright lights. But Mr. Kurnes was different from the doctors and my other teachers. He seemed genuinely interested in me, and he was sensitive to my obvious discomfort.

## When someone believes in you and gives you the chance to be more, take the help because it could change your life

The tests were initially confusing. He had me search through a page on which were printed a series of meaningless letters, characters and symbols. He told me to find groupings of similar characters. After this and some other tests were completed, I was placed in front of a computer, where I had to repeat the sounds generated by the computer of a bunch of "words" that came up on the screen, one after another. What made the exercise challenging was that these "words" were without vowels. Later I progressed to saying actual words, simple ones at first. As the months passed, the exercises became more complex; the words got longer and appeared on the screen faster, and eventually they appeared without audio. At the same time as I was proceeding through these exercises, my grades started to improve.

Not only did I pass every class that year—which in itself was a great accomplishment for me—but I also got two As. For the first time, I realized I was good at math. I even received an award for the highest math mark in my grade. I still have issues with grammar and sentence structure, or "Brammar," as my friends and family call it today. But now, I **understand how to learn**. One thing I have learned is that if you believe, you can achieve. This experience provided me with the resources and dedication to work through my problems, then and in the years that followed. It wasn't that I had mental health issues; it wasn't that I was not intelligent. I had simply not been given the proper foundation for learning.

Always be learning

• • • • •

There is no doubt that this special assistance was instrumental in helping me complete my secondary education. Nonetheless, getting through high school was still a struggle for me. I left home when I was 16 and took a one-bedroom apartment with my older brother only five minutes from our parent's home. Living at home wasn't an option anymore if I wanted to improve my situation. Living with my brother was fun, but challenging because we now had to be self-sufficient.

It was really tough waking up and going to school each morning, but I pushed myself to do it. What else was I going to do every day? Not having a job, I signed up for social assistance—I knew I needed help in supporting myself if I wanted to make it through school. My brother took a different approach: he worked really hard, holding down several jobs at once while still going to school. I was impressed by his determination to build a future without being dependent on the government.

Life in high school was challenging for other reasons. Grades 12 and 13 were especially tough because my brother and I each decided to get our own apartments as our lives were taking us down different paths. Social assistance was enough to cover the rent, but not much else. I was only a teenager, I had never **managed a budget before**, and I spent my money unwisely. Most days, I just didn't have the money to buy enough food, and I had to miss out on school trips and social engagements because I just couldn't afford them. I used to

Learn about budgets/ financials

tell my schoolmates I wasn't into that sort of thing. The truth was I wanted to go so badly I could have cried.

I did attend one school event, though: the blood bank. My desire to get out of class was greater than my fear of needles, so I decided, along with a bunch of friends, to give it a try. After they'd taken all my information, they sat me in an oversized chair. I was just beginning to relax when I saw the nurse approaching me with what appeared to me to be a massive needle. I thought I might faint. The nurse saw my panic and told me there was still time to change my mind, but if I went through with it, I would get to eat cookies and other treats afterward. She had said the magic words. I was so hungry that I forgot my fear and offered up my arm.

After they were finished taking my blood, I moved to the recovery area. Some of my classmates were already at the table with the refreshments, enjoying the treats. Except for my grumbling stomach, I was feeling pretty good, so I decided to stand up and head on over to the table too. When I got there, I reached for a cookie. Then something strange happened. I began to feel tingly all over. I turned to my friend Chris and said I didn't feel well, and the next thing I knew I was lying on the floor with the nurse leaning over me. I had passed out, but that wasn't the worst part. I had eaten only half a cookie, and I was still terribly hungry.

It was hard being hungry all the time, but the loneliness was even worse. Throughout my last two years of high school, I spent almost every night alone in my small, empty apartment, with my empty refrigerator and empty cupboards. More often than not, my unhappiness overwhelmed me. I went to school every day without letting any of my friends know I was living on my own now. I was so afraid of what people would think of me if they knew (and to tell you the truth, I didn't think much of myself either).

Even teenagers who grow up in the most loving households experience emotional turmoil from time to time. The difference is that they typically have someone to talk to. I didn't. I used to get so angry and frustrated at not knowing how to deal with my emotions that I would pound the walls with my fists and scream as loudly as I could. Night after night, I cried myself to sleep. I thought about how my friends and classmates were about to move on to post-secondary schools, where they would surely find excitement and success. For my own future, I could picture nothing beyond the four walls in my empty apartment. It seemed like I would be trapped there forever.

• • • • •

After graduating from high school, I wandered aimlessly through the days. I still knew nothing but poverty and welfare. I had no available financial or personal credit, no formal education other than my high school diploma, no guidance from my family, no career in sight, no financial security, no money in the bank, no direction, and a lot of insecurity. My life seemed like a dead end. To top it off, I was hanging around with the wrong people and ignoring responsibility, hoping success would somehow fall into my lap. I tried a few get-rich-quick schemes before realizing that success doesn't come in a box.

## Success comes to those who are willing to work hard at it. It does not come in the form of a lottery ticket.

There was one scheme I still can't believe I fell for. I especially can't believe that I also tried to do it myself. I read in the paper that I could get up to $1 million in a very short time by sending only $19.99 to the agents at the address provided. They, in turn, promised to send me all the details I needed to get rich. The advertisement assured me it was such a simple idea that I would be shocked. To me, at that time, $20 was lot of money, but I decided to try it anyway and sent the letter with my cash. I checked the mail every day in the week that followed, anxiously waiting for the promised reply. When, at last, I saw the envelope, I admit, my heart started beating faster. What I read when I opened it went something like this: "Thank you for the $19.99. You have helped me get that much closer to reaching my first $1 million. The secret for you to reach your million dollars is to get a post office box so people won't know where you live. Then place an ad in a newspaper, similar to mine.

And then people just like you will start sending you money wanting to know how to make a million dollars."

Everything about this sounded wrong, but, as desperate as I was, I decided to try it. I got a post office box, just as I had been instructed to do, and I placed an advertisement in the paper. For weeks, nothing came in. Then one day I received a letter. It was from someone who had been scammed just like me. The letter-writer told me how upset he was that there were scammers out there who would take advantage of the hopes and dreams of the people who wanted to change their lives.

Success requires hard work

I felt horrible. In my heart of hearts, I also realized that if I was going to be successful **it would take something more than the promise of "success in a box."** Over the years that followed, many people have approached me with various get-quick-rich schemes, telling me, for example, that all I needed to do was enlist between five and 10 of my friends to sell some product or other and get my friends to do the same, and in no time I'd be rich. All I needed to start was to purchase a "starter kit." I eventually realized that it was by selling the starter kits that these companies made money. These businesses that ask you for money up front are usually a form of pyramid scheme—another scam. Like so many lessons, I learned this one the hard way.

I had been living on my own for several years, but when I was 19 I moved in with my younger brother and two of his friends. My roommates were great to be around, but some of the people they associated with were less than ideal companions. Our home ended up being an open house for anyone who wanted to have fun and come and go as they pleased. At first I really enjoyed the environment, but in the end, this was not the life I wanted. But I felt stuck because social assistance made it difficult to find an alternative.

One morning I woke up and just had to get away. I was tired of the revolving door of people coming and going all the time, tired of finding strangers in my house—and sometimes in my room. I was tired of the total lack of respect with which we treated one another, and tired especially with myself for staying. I was tired as well of being poor, of not having a car, of not being able to travel and see the world, of not having a home to call my own. My brother and his two friends also felt this way. We all wanted a better life.

And then it hit me: I didn't have to live like this. Overnight, my perspective changed, and that was the first step towards changing my life. I took my fate into my own hands because I was determined to make something of myself, determined to be more than I had been up to then. There is a saying that I learned much later in life: "If you don't change, you die." Change is an important part of moving forward. If you are standing still, you are actually going backwards. *Keep moving forward* is a phrase I have come to embrace and live by.

# Climbing Out of the Dumpster

2

**TRASH**

# Things Happen for a Reason

My perspective on life had changed overnight, but other changes and success didn't come easily or quickly. I moved out on my own, but I still had very little money, so although I had given up actual dumpster diving a few years earlier when I started living with roommates, I was still a garbage picker. I would sort through furniture and other household items people had put out on the curb as garbage. In fact, I furnished my apartment with items I gathered that way. I would also find items that were gently used, fix them up and sell them as a way of increasing my personal assets. Every time I found something I could use in that way, I would recall that old cliché: one man's trash is another man's treasure.

I did this for years, but eventually I came to a point where I knew it was time to climb out of the dumpster for good. That moment came when a homeowner—a tall man, balding with a large belly, wearing his pajamas—came storming out of his house, screaming at me for going through the furniture he had put out for garbage collection. He was upset that I was looking through his trash—to him, it was an invasion of his privacy. To calm him down, I appealed to his pity; I told him how little money I had, and said I was trying really hard to make something of myself. It worked, and he left me alone, but for the first time I felt ashamed, as though I had cheapened myself simply so I could get some free stuff. I didn't like the feeling, and that was the last time I went dumpster diving. I graduated to thrift stores, where I was able to buy good, professional clothes that provided me with a sense of self-worth and the confidence to set my sights higher than the bottom of garbage bins.

I reconnected with some of the hard-working, responsible and family-oriented friends I'd grown up with but whom I had lost touch with over the years. I got a series of low-paying jobs over the course of eight years: dishwasher, busboy, chamber "maid," labourer, pizza maker, grocery shelf stocker, deliveryman and construction worker, among others. Working in these kinds of jobs was often difficult and frustrating, and I left most of them of my own accord, often when the people I reported to were too closed-minded to consider ideas on how to improve the way of working; instead, they would usually just dismiss me. At times, I became discouraged because these were not the kinds of work I really wanted, but I felt trapped because of my background and education. I wanted to do more, to be more, to be in business and make a difference in the world. So, despite the fatigue, frustration and poverty, I pushed on.

## You might feel trapped because of your experience or education, but if you believe in yourself, anything is possible

Because it was so hard to get the work I wanted, I focused on developing business ideas. If someone wasn't willing to hire me and give me a chance, why not take my own fate into my own hands? One of my first ventures that seemed to have a chance of success was a customer-service company I called Finding Inefficient Gaps Halting Tangible Income Necessary for Growth/Effective Developments Generating positive Experiences—or FIGHTING EDGE. This was back in the early 1990s, when customer service was all the rage. I had worked so many jobs that dealt directly with customers, **I felt sure that I could create a company that would tap into some of my experiences.** I developed a business plan that was weak in many areas only because I did not have the experience necessary to make a convincing plan. My financial sections were there—I

Do what you know

had looked at risks, competitors, marketing, pricing, target audience—but I did not put as much time as I should have into truly understanding the industry. Despite my weak planning, within the first year I had landed several pretty good accounts, including most of the local Subway restaurants, Zellers Portrait Studio, an auto body shop and even a Walmart store at Lincoln Heights Shopping Mall. I dealt with many challenges in this business, from marketing and sales to hiring the people I required to do the evaluations, to finding the money to pay them, to handling client issues. The downfall of the company was my inability to understand how to organize, manage and stay focused when things went awry. When I went off track, I didn't know what to do next. What this and some other start-ups left me with was a better understanding of who I was. I loved being in the middle of the business world, selling and convincing people to work with me, building a new product or service that people would look at and marvel over. This was a sense of accomplishment that would make me feel worthwhile and valued. **The best part of failing is that you learn and move on.** I am the type of person who never quits; when I am faced with failure, I work even harder. I was ready to try again, but I still needed to work in order to pay my bills.

Learn to cope with failure

## Embrace failure, continue to move forward better prepared with lessons learned

I was 24 and still trying to find myself. On a whim, I moved to California to be with a girl, but neither the girl nor the move lasted long. I came back from that adventure in desperate condition, with nothing but my ambition and the clothes on my back. I knocked on the only door I knew would open without question: my grandmother's. As always, she was thrilled to see me. It had been several months since we'd last spoken, and when I asked if I could stay with her for a while, she didn't hesitate for a second. "Of course you can!" And she gave me a big hug, followed by a series of small pats on the back like she used to give me when I was very young. "Let me make you something to eat." It was my childhood days at Grandmother's house all over again.

Honesty builds credibility

I started looking for another job the next day. I padded my resumé with embellishments and references (even though the references had no phone numbers beside them). I will talk later in this book about the **importance of being truthful** and how it seems that most people are dishonest when they talk about their experience and education. I have come to realize that sometimes, when we are starting out, we have no choice. I can't remember how many times I asked someone to "just give me a chance and I will prove what I can do." It was never enough. When you have nothing, padding a resumé doesn't seem that bad. I was comfortable doing it, only because I knew I would be able to back up the credentials I was claiming with the quality of my work and the dedication I would bring to the job. My padding was never really a lie; rather, it involved play on words. For example, instead of saying "Graduated Algonquin College," I would write "Attended Algonquin College." I had attended that college for a year, but never finished. I dropped out because I realized that school was not for me.

Meanwhile, most of my peers were finishing college or university, starting their careers, and I was floating around, trying to get business ideas up and running, and failing over and over. By the time I came back from California and moved in with my grandmother, I didn't care where I worked; I just wanted to get paid.

Soon, I was hired as a waiter at a restaurant near my grandmother's house. It was called Zuma's Rodeo, a nice country-and-western place. One of the hostesses at the restaurant, Nathalie, caught my eye and I fell for her almost immediately. After a month of nervously stammering every time I was in her presence, I got the courage to ask her out. Telephone was the best way, I decided, so I pulled out the phone book and started looking. There were three dozen people in the book with the same last name as Nathalie. I took a deep breath and began dialling. It was absolute torture, but I pushed on. On the ninth call, a woman answered the phone, and when I asked if the Nathalie who worked at Zuma's lived there, I finally got the answer I had been looking for.

When I finally spoke to her, Nathalie agreed to come to a birthday party with me the following Saturday. The night of the party came. I waited for what seemed like ages, but she still hadn't arrived. I was getting nervous. What if she had changed her mind? Then there was a knock at the door. With great anticipation, I opened the door to find a young, frightened teenager waiting outside. Nathalie had sent him. She had been in a traffic accident and was waiting for the police to arrive.

I jumped through the door past the teenager, raced down the street as fast as I could and found Nathalie sitting on the curb, crying. Her car had been sideswiped by a drunk driver when he tried to overtake her on a corner and lost control. Her car was destroyed, but she was okay. As soon as I got there, she fell into my arms and stayed there the whole time the police were questioning her. That was our first date, and the best part of it was that, within the first five minutes, she was already in my arms.

Five months later, I asked Nathalie to marry me. Her parents didn't really approve, and I understood why. Every parent wants the best for their child. I came from a broken home and had neither a career nor any formal education beyond high school. But their disapproval pushed me to better myself even more. I needed to do more, to succeed so I could prove that I was right for their daughter. I needed the stability and focus our marriage would bring. I was determined to work to get more experience and money and build up my personal credibility.

I believe that things happen for a reason. By moving in with my grandmother (after eight years living on my own), I got a job at the restaurant where I would meet my future wife. This would turn out to be one of the most important moments of my life.

Marriage to Nathalie gave my life focus and an extra boost to my determination to do better. She was a strong source of encouragement and support, even though the challenges of our situation in the early years were sometimes tough for her to handle. Unlike me, she had never lived on her own. She had grown up in an environment full of opportunities for her to learn, grow and experience the guidance of a stable family. She never, or rarely, had to pay for anything herself. She wasn't prepared for the day-to-day struggles of paying for food, housing, insurance, car, gas and various other necessities of life. After a couple of months, she broke down and, when I asked her what was wrong, between the sobs she said, "We never have any money. Everything that comes in goes straight to the bills." I had to smile, but she was right. Money was scarce and, unlike me, who had lived with little or no money my entire life, she found it very hard. Living from paycheque to paycheque was not a worry for me. In my experience, struggling was just a part of life.

Despite the newness and stress of these challenges, Nathalie stood by me then, as she has ever since. Throughout our life together, she has constantly supported me in my dreams and business decisions as no one else has done. Meeting her as a result of moving in with my grandmother was a true turning point in my life. But this was not to be the only life-changing development that resulted from this move.

# When Opportunity Knocks

Life sometimes provides us with an opportunity, and it is up to us to decide if we want to make the most of it. If you see an opportunity and decide to take advantage of it, have faith in yourself and go for it. Be prepared to try alternate paths if the one you're on is not working out.

Before the marriage, Nathalie's mother, Lucille, told me about a contract position at the Bank of Canada's call centre. I had always been a "thinker," but to this point all my employment opportunities had taken me to positions of "doer." This, I thought, could be my chance to get the change I wanted and needed, the opportunity to embark on a professional career. Lucille, who had worked at the bank for more than 25 years, helped get me an interview and I got the job, a three-month contract. Now it was up to me to perform and prove myself. Being new, I was given the worst possible shift—noon to eight—but I didn't care. I was so excited to have a "real" job for the first time. I looked forward to building up my resumé and moving on to bigger and better things. Working at the bank was exciting because it was a professional setting that could lead to so much more. Who would have thought that I would be so excited at being able to wear a tie to work?

The excitement didn't last long, however. After two months, I learned that my contract would not be renewed. Even though they said I was one of their best contract employees, they told me they couldn't keep me on because I wasn't bilingual. In situations like this, it's hard not to let your emotions take over. I felt anger and a sense of injustice. I even felt discriminated against. It was hard for me to prove myself to management because my shift and theirs overlapped—they went home at five—so they couldn't really make their decision solely on the basis of my performance.

**Leverage what skills you have**

But instead of focusing on what I lacked, **I tried to find things that would make me stand out from all the rest**.

It became really hard for me to concentrate on my work. One evening, while I was waiting for a call to come in, I noticed a flip chart and I started to doodle on it. I wondered what kinds of things I could doodle that would get noticed. If it was just a random image, no one would really care, but if I doodled things related to work, I knew that they would get noticed. I did not know what the outcome would be, but what did I have to lose? Night after night, I had been talking to prospective purchasers about how Canada Savings Bonds were the building blocks of our future, so I thought I would draw something related to this. My pictures began with the words CANADA SAVINGS BONDS all stacked on top of each other in a thick box-like line. I would then fill in the words so that the series of them looked like a wall of bricks. The idea was to have the words "Canada Saving Bonds" over top of the word "Future" and, across the top of the picture, the statement "CSB are the building blocks for our futures." I spent a lot of time on the details of the picture—shadowing, highlighting brick details and getting the 3D look and feel so that when people looked at it, they'd believe it.

My drawings were well received by my co-workers, so I doodled some more. Each night, I posted a new collage outside the main elevators for all to see. What I did not expect is that they were never taken down. I even heard that one of the directors from another floor had mentioned them during a meeting. These little sketches were starting to draw attention, and they became my only hope that I would be kept on at the bank. With only two weeks left in my contract, I put even more time and effort into continuing to produce them.

People started to talk, and eventually everyone knew that I was the secret doodler. My boss approached me to say that she wanted me to make more for other floors in the building, so I did, and this time I signed them. Just before the end of my contract period, she approached me again, and this time offered me a one-year contract. She told me she was impressed by my initiative and, despite the language barrier, they saw that I had potential. I had gained their respect, and they had decided I was worth keeping, even though I didn't know French.

I worked hard the following three years. I took on any job I was asked to do. I came in at night and on weekends. I switched shifts with others when they asked me to and eagerly assumed new responsibilities when I got the chance. My willingness to do so much allowed me to gain knowledge comparable to that of some of the more senior people in the department. Partly in recognition of the contribution I was making to the department, I was put on a three-day-per-week schedule. I was getting a full salary for a short work week, but with long days. These positions were usually offered only to the more experienced members of staff because you had to be able to answer questions about all the bank's product lines when there was no one around but you with the information.

This was good, but it was not enough. I was hungry to climb the corporate ladder, so when a management position became available, I applied for it. I had all the requisite qualifications and more, and I was confident I would get an interview. My confidence was justified and I was excited, and yet nervous at the prospect. This was my opportunity to get into management! Well, the interview did not go the way I thought it would. I had the qualifications and the experience, all right, but my downfall was my inability to speak French fluently. I could speak it, but not that well. The position required that the manager be able to deal with customers in both English and French. I didn't get the job.

Once I understood that my lack of fluency in Canada's second official language was going to keep me from ever being promoted within the department, I asked my manager if she would sign a release to allow me to apply for other jobs within the bank. To my surprise, she refused. My willingness to work hard, to gain the knowledge and take on additional responsibilities had made me too valuable to the department. They could not afford to give me up. After several weeks of discussion, both with my manager and with the departmental director, in which they persisted in refusing to release me, I handed in my resignation. Did I want to quit? Absolutely not! **But I did want to control my own fate.** I could not allow someone else to determine how my career would progress. To say that my manager

Believe in
your abilities

was shocked by my decision would be an understatement. She tried hard to convince me to stay, but unless they were willing to change their rules and let me take on a role somewhere else in the bank, I was on my way out the door.

During my last two weeks at the bank, I spent a lot of time looking for work. I finally found an opportunity with a friend who owned a small graphic design company. Bill's company, FYT Graphics, did work for people and companies looking for quick turnaround on basic designs. After a brief discussion with Bill and an investment of $2,500, I became an equal partner in FYT. My time with Bill would prove to be valuable, not only from a creative standpoint, but also from a business one.

I worked with Bill for close to a year, learning how to design using tools such as Photoshop and Corel Draw. I also learned that in order to be successful, we needed to have more business. I had assumed that my role in FYT would be to bring in more business— that my focus would be on the sales side. I talked to Bill about how we could increase our sales and how we might be able to grow the business. I felt our biggest challenge was visibility: our workspace was located inside a professional photography studio on the second floor of an old building. It was a nice spot, but in order to grow, we needed to get out of there. Because our money was limited, I looked at what we could do that was inexpensive. This came down to media and signage. I placed ads in local papers. I also decorated my white station wagon with the FYT name. This was my first car, and I was really proud of it. Painting it like that was hard, but I reckoned it would help get additional exposure for our company.

Still, we were not really getting anywhere with business development. I convinced Bill that we had to look at what value proposition we had that made us different. I talked about moving our office to a corner location, at ground level. The idea was to create a coffee shop and one-stop shop for film development. If we installed a new film-processing machine that could turn around rolls of film within 20 minutes, customers could patronize the retro coffee shop while they waited. I scoped out the perfect location. Part of the new space would be set aside for our design business but we would do more. My partner indicated that he was on board with the concept—**or so I thought**—and I

Ensure expectations are aligned

spent close to three months building the business plan, meeting with suppliers for tables, chairs, coffee essentials, film and equipment. I designed the layout of the space, the marketing strategies, and signage for the external windows. I even spent several days out on the corner, counting passersby and traffic outside our future front door. When the negotiations with suppliers and the landlord were complete, I sat down with my partner to discuss our move and the way forward. To my surprise, he said he wanted no part of my plan.

The worst part was that he always knew he didn't want to take part in this project. He felt it was risky. He liked our current business model, which was having fun and making a little money. There is nothing wrong with this, of course, but I was on a different path. I wanted to build something bigger. At the end of our first year together, we separated on good terms. Bill and I are still close friends, but our business needs were just too different. Still, in my time at FYT, I learned a lot about design and got an introduction to what it means to be part of a business team. When I look back at our time together, I don't think I would change anything.

## Things will not always go the way you want them to, so focus on the positives that will help you keep moving forward

I needed to find work again. Nathalie and I were expecting our first baby. I could not afford not to be making money, so I looked to the only place where I had experience: the bank. As it happened, and somewhat unexpectedly, the only job available was in a department that required proficiency only in English. The position was the lowest-grade job at the bank, but I knew that if I could get the opportunity, I would shine and get to where I knew I always belonged: in a position of leadership. When I got an interview, one of the first questions they asked me was why I was applying. I had much more experience than the job required, and they **were concerned I would feel it was beneath me**. I told them that I knew the pay level was less than

Be willing to do anything

what I had been making before with the bank, but that it was in a department I knew I could excel in, and that I would give them 110 per cent effort to make sure I did this job as well as it could be done. After I was hired, I performed as I had promised I would: not only did I do the job well, but I also worked hard, put in late nights and weekends, and developed ways to make the department more efficient.

I presented my ideas to my manager on a regular basis, and she would often tell me that this was not part of my responsibilities. She was actually a year younger than me, and it seemed as though she was threatened by my eagerness and my drive to succeed. She would often scold me, in a polite way, about being so focused on my work. I always finished my work much earlier then was required. I was data-processing financial information from other banks across the country, and the job was quite simple and repetitive. I ended up creating several automated tools to help me process and present the data at our weekly meetings. These presentations were made not only to my manager, but to *her* manager as well. He was always complimenting me on my initiative while she would sit there, looking grim. I didn't care. I was focused on my goals of growing within the department and being able to support my family.

Within six months of my return to the bank, an opening came up for an upper management role, one (again) that did not require mastery of the French language. The position was in my old department, but two levels more senior than the job I had applied for a year and half before. It was for a program manager to oversee all the projects in the department and provide support to the project teams. But before I could even apply for the position, I needed my manager to sign a release. I approached her apprehensively to ask for her approval. After she read the job description, she observed that the position was several management levels higher than hers, and that no one in at level 9 had ever jumped to level 15 before. She laughed and said, "Why not give it a try?" This was her way of putting me in my place. If I didn't get the position, she would take pleasure in my discomfiture. I had no intention of giving her that satisfaction.

The main impediment, from my point of view, was that the job required someone with experience in project management, which

I did not have. I was great at customer service. **What I needed to do was learn project management— and quickly.**

Be able to adapt

A benefit of working at the bank was that they had a learning centre where anyone could pick up new skills on their own time. Project management software was one of the tools that they provided training on. So I applied for the management position and then spent nights and weekends learning everything I could about project management. Several weeks after I submitted my application, I received a call inviting me for a first interview with the director's management team. Each member of the team would ask me questions. About what, I wasn't sure, but I was confident that I would be prepared. I had three years of experience in the department, had been studying project management for close to two weeks straight, and was eager to show all the things I did to stand out and advance my department. The interview took about 10 minutes. It was really just a quick test to see if I had the basic qualifications for the job. They mentioned it would be a three-round interview process and that 67 other candidates had applied for the job. Weeks passed and I heard nothing. My manager, seeming to gloat a little, told me she wasn't surprised I hadn't been called, considering the gap between my present level and the one I was aiming for. I was discouraged, but kept my head about me and continued to study project management. I am glad I did.

Shortly after her jibe, I was called for a second interview, this time to meet two of the senior managers, who were going to ask me about my project management experience and skills. I had no formal skills, but from an experience perspective, having run a business (which is like running a project), I was not without relevant experience. I was planning on pulling from that experience to support my answers. The two managers asked me about project management terminology, processes, and the software they used, and I was able to respond without delay and with confidence. Did I really know as much as I let on? Not at all! But I had been studying for weeks and was ready for the interview. Preparation is one of the key factors leading to success.

During the second interview, the managers indicated that the selection process was now down to fewer than 10 people, including me. They said that if I got another interview it would be with the departmental director and head of finance. As I returned to my desk, I thought about whom I would be meeting with and decided I would ask people around the office what they knew about the director and what he liked and disliked, his habits and interests, and so on. I found out he had written a paper on management versus leadership, which I found and read. I also discovered that he liked sports, including badminton, which I also enjoyed—I had helped coach our high school badminton team. I had no idea if I would get to use this information, but I was determined to be ready if I got the chance.

## Working hard will lead to opportunities if you keep your eye out for them

I was the only person in the office, or so I thought, on a Sunday about three weeks later, when out of a corner office came the director of my department. He walked over to my desk and said he was having computer problems and asked if I could help. I proceeded to fix his computer; he thanked me and I returned to my desk. About an hour later, he again approached my desk and asked what I was doing in the office on a Sunday. I explained that I was working to help improve my job and the efficiencies of the department. He asked what my level was, which I thought was an odd question. I told him that although I was a level 9, I actually worked at a much higher level. I went on to tell him the story of my time at the bank, and about the job I had applied for, but didn't get. He was impressed that I was there on a Sunday and went on to say that he was playing badminton with the director of the other department I had applied to the next day and promised to mention me. Was his intervention decisive? I don't know, but I got a third interview.

It turned out that the director who was doing the hiring had not yet made a decision. Now it was down to me and a woman who had 15 years' experience at the bank. The director's main concern about my candidacy was that I would be responsible for managing my old managers from my previous job, as some of them would be involved in project work. He asked how I would deal with that challenge. My response must have impressed him, because he hired me. I started the following week in the POD group (Planning, Organization and Development). It was ironic that a year and half earlier I had been arguing with my managers to allow me to take on a managerial role, and now, after leaving the bank and coming in through another department, I was able to grow not only into a managerial role, but one in my previous department. Since this was upper management, I did not have to work directly with the public, which meant that French was not required. My hard work and persistence had paid off. Five years after starting at the bank, I was responsible for overseeing 13 projects as part of the bank's senior management's planning department and managing many teams, including people who were once my supervisors.

As a full-time manager with the bank, I was given the opportunity to take external courses to help advance my knowledge and increase my efficiency. Even though the policy allowed staff members to take only two courses per year, in my final year with the bank I managed to attend more than a dozen. They let me do this, I think, because I was eager to acquire as much knowledge as I could, now that I had the opportunity. More importantly, from the bank's point of view, every time I returned from a course **I made sure my new-found knowledge trickled down to my project teams** so that we were all becoming more efficient.

Never burn your bridges

For example, I took several courses to learn how to use Microsoft Project. This taught me how to integrate a number of projects into one common updating system. This system enabled me to send a status update request that would prompt anyone on any of the 13 projects I supervised to provide me with an update on their progress. (This was, of course, before online project management systems became available.) When you are looking at thousands of tasks across that many projects, it is daunting to have to make those requests one at a time, on an individual basis. In order to make my new system work, I had to install software components on all my team members' computers. Most employees were annoyed that I was spending so much time implementing this new management system, but once it was completed they all realized the benefits. My boss was impressed, and I was able to convince him to send me on more courses. I was building on my skills, and he was getting a great deal: it was a win-win situation.

During my time with the bank, I was building up a professional career, but not gaining much personal credibility. Sometimes, discussions with senior management would shift away from work-related topics to the economy, fiscal policies or politics, and when that happened I noticed that my comments were often ignored. I had the impression that this was because I didn't have a post-secondary degree or any of the other, similar credentials most people there had. I decided to look for credibility from other sources. Drawing on what I had learned about project management technology, I submitted a proposal to speak at a conference at the Ottawa Congress Centre, one of the city's largest event halls. To my surprise, I was selected. My topic was "Project Management Software: How It Can Help Us and How It Can Hurt Us." This was my first time speaking in front of a large group of my peers, 100 of them. For the most part, these were individuals experienced and educated in project management—not like me, just taking a course on the subject now

Overcome your personal fears

and then. It's not an exaggeration to say I was terrified. I could hardly sleep at all for weeks prior to the lecture. I had heartburn all the time and kept thinking up excuses to get out of having to do it. **I had to keep telling myself over and over that I could do it, that I needed to do it in order to start building personal credibility.** I was very scared, but I was also very determined. I needed to face my fears, and I did.

At the time, I had no idea where that experience would take me. Halfway through my speech, someone in the audience asked me a question, which to this day I can't recall, but I do remember that I did not know the answer to it and I actually blanked out. I completely lost my train of thought. I started feeling really hot, as if the sun were beating down only on me, and then my eyes began tearing up. It felt as if I had gone silent for a very long time and that everyone was staring, wondering what I was doing, but in reality only a few seconds passed before I recovered. I focused on a couple of audience members and pulled myself together, and, according to some feedback I got later, my lecture was a success.

Not only did that event increase my credibility, it also provided the opportunity for me to meet Scott Hunter, an experience that significantly changed my life. Scott was the president of a local project management firm called the Project Management Centre (PMC). He told me he was impressed by what he had heard from his business partner, who had been in the audience, and that he wanted to offer me a job working for him as a project management consultant, a position that would pay double what I was making at the bank and would provide me with opportunities to work within multiple industries.

As I had previously learned, gaining varied experiences was invaluable if I wanted to grow professionally. This was perfect timing for me; my wife and I were expecting our first child. It was an opportunity I couldn't pass up, and it eventually led to even more opportunities. Several years after being employed with PMC, I was able to leverage the flexibility of my consulting time to build my first company, EasyWrapLines—all with Scott's approval, as he was my employer. As a consultant with PMC, I helped organizations become more efficient by leveraging the discipline of project management. I was good at this job and worked on many different projects over my two years with the firm. I would meet with the project teams and we would walk through their plans together, assessing what they had accomplished to date and figuring out where they seemed to have run aground. Sometimes I saw the problem right away. On other occasions, it required a number of meetings and a fair bit of diligence to arrive at a solution. In almost all cases the main problems had to do with planning—or its absence. By 2002–2003 I had left PMC to start my own company, EasyWrapLines. Close to seven years later, Scott and I became business partners in another venture. That led to the development of my second business, iPal Interactive Learning, which was later acquired by another company, and Scott became one of my senior management team members with our new employer. It is amazing how life can play out.

From the moment on that morning in my late teens when the thought hit me, "I don't have to live like this anymore," I began to take steps to climb out of that dead-end dumpster-diving existence. Each step forward led to another opportunity, allowing me to build on my success each time. In order to take such steps, however, one needs to be able to recognize opportunities even when they are not obvious, and to leverage them into success. Fortunately, I was able to do that.

# 3

# Becoming an Entrepreneur

# A Good Entrepreneur

**Being a good entrepreneur calls for a combination of strong personal characteristics and professional skills.**

I heard one of the "sharks" on the TV show *Shark Tank* recently refer to a contestant who was making a pitch for investment as a "wantrepreneur." The contestant, who was supposed to be an entrepreneur, had started a business and was now in front of these investors asking not only for money, but also for someone else to do the company's selling, team building and all-round business development. That person had the notion that all it took to be an entrepreneur was an idea. But, of course, that is only the beginning. It takes much more than wanting to be an entrepreneur to actually be one and to turn your idea into a business success.

As we will see throughout this chapter—and indeed, it is a theme of the whole book—a combination of professional skills and personality traits are required to be an entrepreneur. By way of a brief summary, the following are some of those that will help you start, develop and sustain your business successfully. This list is not intended to be exhaustive.

## Determination

There will always be times when things seem to be taking too long to progress, and even some occasions when you may feel that you will never get ahead. As an entrepreneur, these moments can take a toll on your bank account, your mental stability and your patience. During these times, it is important to remain determined and focused on your goals.

## Persuasiveness

You must be able to communicate in a way that will make people understand and support your vision. This means being able to paint a good picture in order to show those whose help, cooperation or business you need, the path you intend to follow. Plans don't matter if you can't convince anyone to believe in you.

## Problem-solving ability

In business, new problems arise constantly. It is important to approach each problem with ready and real solutions, and a good dash of patience. If you can only identify problems and cannot find solutions, you will struggle as an entrepreneur.

## Creativity

The ability to think creatively is a strong asset in most areas of business activity, particularly in solving problems. Creative solutions to problems often require you to visualize processes, partnerships, presentations and results. Converting problems into creative solutions will help you leverage opportunities much more easily.

## Coping ability

An entrepreneurial career is a high-stress career. You need to be able to cope with limited resources, conflicts and uncertainty. If stress causes your temper to explode or triggers a mental breakdown, this might not be the job path for you.

## Multi-tasking ability

In overseeing day-to-day operations and in developing new business opportunities, you will be constantly called on to move between various deliverables, groups and resources. You must be able to manage multiple tasks or you will always be running into delays, shortfalls and other avoidable problems.

## Risk awareness

Risk is an inevitable part of entrepreneurship, and it can be your best friend. Paying careful attention to risk forces you to consider the worst-case scenario and understand the challenges you face. Once you understand them, you can avoid being caught off guard and plan mitigation strategies to overcome or weaken their effects.

## Openness to learning

Being open to learning continually, rather than thinking you already know everything you need to know to develop your business, is one of the more useful characteristics of the good entrepreneur. This is especially important when it comes to the need to learn from mistakes, because mistakes will certainly be made.

# A Good Entrepreneur

In becoming an entrepreneur, there is no single element that will make you successful; it is a combination of many of them. Entrepreneurship is learning to figure things out. What this model tells you is that a good entrepreneur is determined, open to learning, persistent and so much more. If you are not strong in certain areas (such as creativity), but are strong in others (such as problem-solving abilities), you will most likely find someone who can complement your strengths and weaknesses. That is what it is all about. You need to be able to figure out who you are, what your limitations are and what would make you a good entrepreneur.

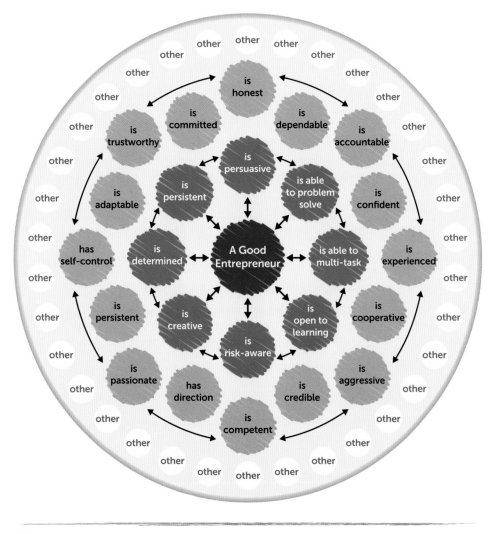

MODEL #2

# Becoming an Entrepreneur

**Before you start:** It is critical that, before you dive headfirst into becoming an entrepreneur, you first understand what you will have to deal with. Here is a simple process that I created to guide you through your decisions.

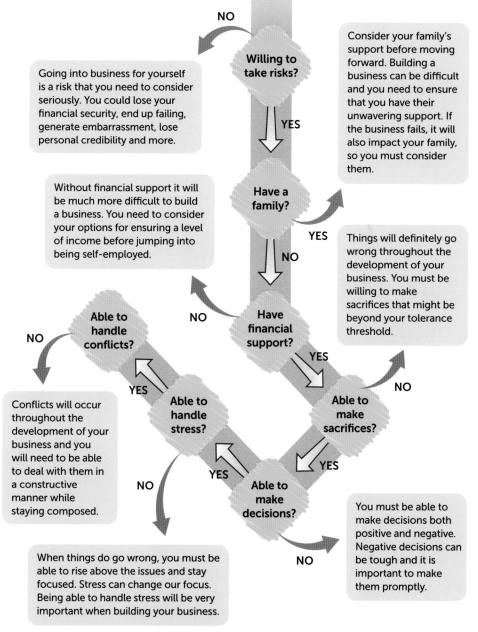

NO

**Willing to take risks?**

Consider your family's support before moving forward. Building a business can be difficult and you need to ensure that you have their unwavering support. If the business fails, it will also impact your family, so you must consider them.

Going into business for yourself is a risk that you need to consider seriously. You could lose your financial security, end up failing, generate embarrassment, lose personal credibility and more.

YES

**Have a family?**

Without financial support it will be much more difficult to build a business. You need to consider your options for ensuring a level of income before jumping into being self-employed.

YES

NO

Things will definitely go wrong throughout the development of your business. You must be willing to make sacrifices that might be beyond your tolerance threshold.

**Able to handle conflicts?**

NO

**Have financial support?**

NO

YES

**Able to make sacrifices?**

NO

YES

**Able to handle stress?**

YES

NO

Conflicts will occur throughout the development of your business and you will need to be able to deal with them in a constructive manner while staying composed.

YES

**Able to make decisions?**

NO

You must be able to make decisions both positive and negative. Negative decisions can be tough and it is important to make them promptly.

When things do go wrong, you must be able to rise above the issues and stay focused. Stress can change our focus. Being able to handle stress will be very important when building your business.

NO

Being an entrepreneur and choosing to start up a business is not an easy decision. Most who do decide to try it fail. Aside from asking yourself if you have what it takes to handle the long hours, the hard work and the stress, you also have to consider how the move would affect your life and your family. If you have a family when you decide you want to go into business for yourself, it would be a good idea to have the conversation about it with your spouse before taking the plunge. The decision will impact not just your life, but the lives of those you care about, and their support will be ever valuable, especially during difficult times. In addition, you not only need to plan for the business, you also need to plan, as much as you can, for your life. What will you do if things do not go as you expected they would? And above all, do you have supportive people around you who will stick by you during both the good times and the bad?

# Getting Started: Finding Your Vision

Having a vision of what you want to build will help get you on your way to building it. Like a puzzle, a business has many pieces that need to be put together in the right way in order to complete the picture. If you know what you have to create and follow a process, you will be able to complete the puzzle much more easily.

Although for many years I wasn't sure what I wanted to do with my life, I knew that, at heart, I was an entrepreneur. I guess you could say I've always been an entrepreneur. Even as a child, I was thinking of new and creative ways to make money. Winter was always my favourite season, because that's when I would go door to door, offering to shovel my neighbours' driveways. That little venture ended up teaching me one of my first big business lessons. If I charged a fixed rate—say, five dollars—my customers would never pay me more than that. However, if I told them they could pay whatever they liked (like a donation), they would usually give me more—$10, sometimes even more.

Later, I discovered a new venture that was, perhaps, less lucrative but certainly more creative: rooting out from underneath vending machines the loose change that people had dropped when they were buying their treats. For those people, it wasn't worth the effort to reach in under the machine just to retrieve a few quarters, but I, a young teen with little or no money, was only too happy to do so. My brothers and I soon developed a system to scoop up the change more efficiently, and we would use it at every machine we saw. Later, we applied this system to an even bigger source of change: the arcades. The arcades were more rewarding, but because the machines there had to be tipped over before we could get underneath them, they also were more challenging. It required at least two people to do this task, and my brothers were more than happy to help out. This was when I first learned that you could accomplish more when people work together. With the money we earned, we would buy toys and candy, and sometimes even play those same arcades that we mined for change.

I didn't think in those terms at the time, of course, but in a small way I was already expressing my basic entrepreneurial nature. From the beginning, I had always liked the idea of working for myself, being in charge of my own destiny and having the flexibility that goes with entrepreneurship. I also had the notion that someday I would build my own business. During my last year of high school, we were all asked to write something about a close friend of ours to include later in our final yearbook. My friend Chris wrote about me. I didn't see it at the time, but when the yearbook came out I saw that he had written, "Knowing Brad, he will probably end up being the founder and president of some international company." Interesting that people saw that potential in me even in high school.

My Yearbook Photograph

I had read when I was young that many very successful people had achieved their success through businesses built on the principle of economies of scale. They produced and sold a large number of the same product, thereby reducing the costs per unit and simplifying distribution. I had this idea in the back of my mind for years and was looking for a product I could apply it to.

One day, I was shopping at The Bay and bought a sweater for my wife. Never a person who likes to wrap gifts, I went to the wrapping department to get a decorative box that I could simply put the sweater in and add a bow to. There were all sorts of decorative gift bags and wrapping papers, but no boxes that didn't have The Bay's

See opportunities where others do not

logo on them. I went from store to store, looking for a decorative box that didn't have a company logo on it, but couldn't find one. It was then that the light went on! **This was the product on which I could build a business employing the principle of economies of scale.** I would develop a business producing and selling decorative gift boxes and related paper products. This may seem like a very basic idea, but the principle behind it could lead to millions of dollars in revenue.

## The idea for a business could come to you from anywhere, but an idea is nothing without a vision

In some ways, building a business is like putting together a puzzle. You can't just start ramming pieces together, with no idea of what you're doing or without a concept of the final product, hoping they'll somehow all fit just fine. To have some idea of what you're putting together, and how to go about doing it, you need to see a picture of what the finished product should look like. In business, that picture or concept is called your "vision." I now had the vision for my first successful business—the fundamental idea of what I wanted that business to be. To determine what your vision will be, you must look at what you want to get out of your business. Why are you building your product or service? What are you hoping to accomplish when you are successful? When people look at your company, what do you want them to ultimately say about it?

# Piecing Together a Puzzle

As with putting together a puzzle, planning your steps before you start, focusing first on the pieces or small sections rather than the big picture, will help you overcome the fear of taking on the large, complicated project of building your business.

It is one thing to have the vision, quite another to turn it into a concrete business reality. One of the biggest stumbling blocks people face when thinking of taking on a big project is fear—fear of the sheer size of the venture, fear of insufficient time and money, fear of the unknown. These fears stem mainly from inexperience and lack of knowledge of how to proceed with the job. **The key to overcoming them is planning.**

Planning is the foundation

As with putting together a puzzle, in developing any business or idea, it's crucial that you plan your steps before moving forward. To get to your goal, you simply have to take it one piece at a time. When we focus on the pieces, or small sections of similar pieces, organizing them into manageable groups, the task doesn't look so scary anymore. At the beginning, the task can seem overwhelming, but after a while, patterns start to emerge and the picture begins to take shape. Along the way, there will always be challenges that hinder the progress. Almost certainly, in putting together a business, one of the big ones will be accessing sufficient money to hire the right people, market your product or service, attend trade shows to network and make contacts, etc. To get adequate financial backing, you need to convince people that, despite limitations, you really are able to make things happen. But first you have to believe it yourself. Your ability to succeed is within you. You are the one with all the pieces, and you are the one who can see the bigger picture. It's all about working with the resources you have and bringing them together to make up for those you haven't yet attained.

As I was about to plan and start my first business, it seemed that I didn't have much to work with other than belief in myself. I knew that I needed to plan my processes and organize my thoughts. I would have to leverage everything I could in order to expand my options and maximize the results. Without formal post-secondary education, I wouldn't have known where to begin except for an interesting article I had read some years earlier in the magazine *Entrepreneur*. The piece was about project management and how, through proper project management skills, a project manager was able to successfully complete a major project and save his organization millions of dollars in the process. Even as I read, I still wasn't sure what project management was, but if it could help me formalize my thoughts and enable me to not make as many mistakes as I felt I was making, I would spend the time to learn more—and luckily enough, while at the bank I had the opportunity. And I did. Not only did I embrace project management after that day and effectively use it in my management career and business developments over the years, but by the end of 2010, I had worked my way up to becoming a board member and then one of Ottawa's youngest Project Management Institute chapter presidents, overseeing several thousand members, 60-plus volunteers and a board of directors consisting of 11 members.

## Complexity can be organized and more easily understood through planning

For me, project management was the key to putting all the pieces of my business puzzle together. This methodology took the lessons I'd learned from my life experience and translated them into a format that made me a better businessperson. It made me realize more than ever that planning is absolutely critical to succeeding in business. I learned the techniques of properly developing a project, watching the risks and developing communication and negotiating strategies. **I learned how to organize my thought processes and establish the discipline required to be more successful.** Since my visions

You must have good organizational skills

have always been rather grand, these skills have been especially helpful. When I set out to develop a business idea, I think in terms of selling globally, not just locally. Most people would tell me that I was dreaming, that thinking that big was unrealistic, that I needed to think small at first and then I could eventually grow larger. But whether you plan small or big, you need to start small anyway, so why not plan from the outset for where you really want to go? I knew that if I could just organize my thoughts better, I would be able to not only plan big but accomplish big as well. Project management helped me to achieve that.

# All the Chips Are In

> Taking risks is an integral part of being in business for yourself. If you are not willing to put everything on the line and take the risks that others might not be willing to take, reconsider this career path.

Going into business is a gamble. In a poker game, it's okay to bluff, or to put all the chips in the pot, even when you have a bad hand. In fact, it makes you a better poker player. Business isn't like that. In business, you have to make sure you have a great hand before deciding to go all in.

Yes, you will need to take risks—perhaps, sometimes, even big ones—but your risks can be mitigated if you are planning out your game. Just like in poker, your game improves if you understand what makes a good hand. If you are new to poker and don't really understand the rules, you will most likely lose before you even start. There are, of course, those lucky individuals who somehow make it through a few hands and even come out the winner, but these situations are very rare.

In order to be good in business you must understand how to increase your chances of winning by better understanding the rules, what you need to know to increase your chances of improving your hand, and how to read your opponents. When you are starting your business, you need to have some indicators that you have something you can play with. You should not go into business without validation that you are addressing a need or solving a problem. A business usually becomes successful because people see the need for your product or service. It fills a gap that the consumers might not even have known they wanted filled.

So what makes a great hand? There are at least three elements.

First, a product or service that has received positive response. This means you have discussed your idea with people in the industry, family, friends and business professionals, and most of them say that your product or service is something that could do very well. Others are validating that you have something to build on. There may be skeptics who, though they like your idea, go on to say that there would eventually be too much competition or that it would take a lot to get your idea off the ground. But the important thing is that they like the idea. If every person you show your idea to says it is not a good one, perhaps you had better rethink it.

## Your product or service should solve a problem or address a need if you want to increase your chance for success

Second, a product or service that has potential for growth and bringing in revenue. So you have a great idea that people like, but what about its ability to grow your sales? Perhaps you have a product that is made for a specific target market only. This might reduce your chances of success if that market is not interested in your line. There are a lot of great ideas, but if the market is so small that the chance for growth and increased revenues is limited, the risks might be too high to proceed with it. Perhaps you are looking at building a very small business for yourself, with no interest in or possibility of national or international opportunities. That is okay, but you should be aware of that prior to starting your business.

Third, success as defined by you. This ties into the last point. You should be the one who defines what success will mean for you. If you are looking to develop a small, localized business and that is all you really want, then go for it. If you are looking to grow your business to be global, then that is okay as well, but this would mean different levels of planning and risks that you will have to consider before you start. Either way, the scope of the business you want to build will determine the level of work involved in developing it. I have built several businesses, and **success for me was when I felt I was able to take care of my family financially**. In my view, building and selling the business was the goal. Success is what makes you happy. In my case, ensuring my family's future and providing opportunities to my children that I never had growing up is success.

You define success

Even with a good hand, when you decide to start moving forward with your idea, be aware that you will be required to take chances and risks, and while the outcomes could be favourable, they might not. There will be many factors influencing the outcome. You will make mistakes and, hopefully, learn from them. The stress level will be very high. As in playing poker, some people can handle the pressure, others cannot. To a great extent, your success as an entrepreneur will depend on whether you know what you are doing, how well prepared you are and your openness to learning as you progress.

# Poetry, Notebooks and Whiteboards

As an entrepreneur, I continually think about all aspects of my business development. There are countless thoughts that race through my mind on how to improve my business, how to grow into new markets, how to support my team and how to solve the many challenges that arise. When I imagine myself going back to the time when I was an insecure teenager, I remember that my thoughts centred on my feeling of being alone, the constant fear of failure and, of course, dealing with the normal emotional turmoil that goes with being young. Dealing with these feelings and thoughts was especially challenging and frustrating because I didn't have a method for communicating them. I had never

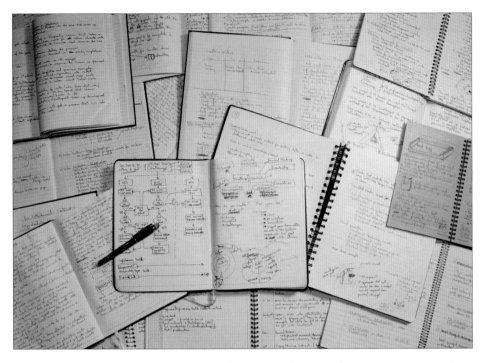

You can't remember everything. Get it on paper, in your tablet, on a whiteboard and continue to build from it. You can always refer back to your notes later on.

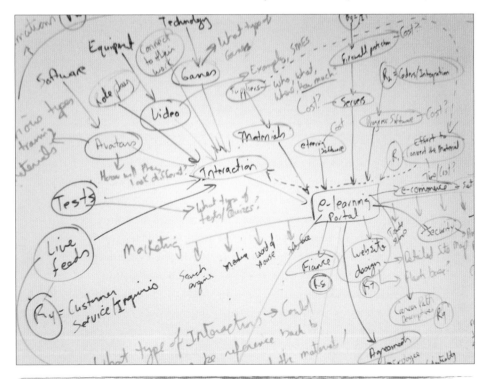

written down my thoughts before. When I started to do this, I noticed that I felt much better, and in the end it helped clear and focus my mind.

The simple process of writing poetry helped me work through many struggles and set a pattern that still forms part of my approach to problem-solving to this day. An additional benefit to my poetry writing was that it resulted in the development of over a hundred poems and, being an entrepreneur, I decided to create a business leveraging them. I called this fledgling business Feelings. It consisted of soaking my printed poems in tea, baking them in the oven and burning the edges with a lighter to give them an old-fashioned look. I would then roll each burnt poem into a scroll and finish them with a red ribbon. These would then be tied together with a rose and sold at flower shops. I was only 18 years old at the time and didn't have much experience in manufacturing. After I received my first order for more than 200 scrolls, I soon realized that baking and burning tea paper in a house with room-mates wasn't the best idea. I created so much smoke that our fire alarm kept going off!

Even though I continue to write poetry today, I have expanded my habit of writing things down to include notebooks and the use of whiteboards, and this has become part of my daily working procedure. Over the years, I have accumulated more than 10 books of notes containing my business ideas, processes, models, theories and solutions to problems. Being able to move my thoughts to paper helped me move my thinking forward and in a much more controlled manner. Using whiteboards also helps keep key topics top of mind and always visible for me to improve upon and move forward into a more formal piece of work.

Today, I have many whiteboards in my offices. **I encourage my teams to use whiteboards as often as possible to work through their ideas and to help them formulate solutions.** Having your thoughts written out and left in plain sight for others to see also helps stimulate conversation, which tends in turn to result in more collaboration.

Write down thoughts

# Planning: The Foundation of Success

Of all the elements of project management, the most important is planning. Good, thorough, step-by-step planning is the best way to ensure you start your business on a solid foundation and get it on the road to success. Lack of sufficient planning will likely lead to many unnecessary headaches down the road.

The main focus of project management, as the name suggests, is typically on project initiatives, but I have found that the principles employed can be effective for all types of business ideas and developments.

I built my businesses by following and customizing the methodologies of project management to meet my needs. Project management involves planning, organizing, securing and managing resources to help you achieve specific goals. To me, the most important of these is planning, the foundation on which project management is based.

I find it amazing to hear people say they do not see value in planning. When I hear this, I can only think it's for one of two reasons: either they do not understand the benefits of planning and the advantages they would have if they only took the time to think through what they wanted to do before setting out to do it, or they are the kind of people who are focused on get-rich-quick schemes and are only interested in trying to do things the easy way. Many people think that if they only had the money, they would be able to make things happen right away. Money is a huge benefit, for sure, but if you don't have the plans in place, there is a very good chance you will simply burn through the money and accomplish very little. Planning is not meant to take time away from the really important things. It is meant to ensure that the important things are done right the first time so that you won't have to redo them or end up making costly preventable mistakes.

Planning isn't wish fulfillment. It is a step-by-step organizing process, a way of thinking through what you would like to do and figuring out how to do it. It takes time and a lot of effort, to be sure, but in the long run it will save time and unnecessary effort. The planning process can be as simple as sticking on a Post-It note or as complicated as completing a 500-page document. It could involve outlining risks, technical specifications, quality standards, communication strategies and much more, but the principles are the same.

## Taking the time to plan today will save you many failures that could happen tomorrow

When I was younger, I did not have formal training in planning, and that turned out to be a big weakness when I was attempting to build my businesses. I tried to develop plans, but I did not follow them through to completion. I would get confused about what I had to do next. I would skip steps because I did not understand why they were needed and I would cut corners to speed up the process of getting to results. What happened instead was that I ended up facing many more challenges, and losing productivity because of the time spent overcoming problems. **Only when I embraced project management and truly understood how to plan did I succeed at business.**

Planning saved me time and money

Over the years, I came to see planning as the key to solid business development, the foundation of success. As with putting together a puzzle, at the beginning you see the overall picture, the vision, in your mind, but you don't dive in and begin assembling the pieces in any old way. You first take a good look at different sections of the big picture and do some grouping, organizing and planning on how best to proceed.

Or, to take another analogy, in constructing a house, you start with the foundation. Without this, you cannot build the walls, the roof and so forth. Planning is the solid base on which you successfully put together the other components of your business. Every good business has a plan. The stronger your plan, the greater your chance of success. As the old saying goes, "If you fail to plan, you plan to fail."

# Take one day at a time!

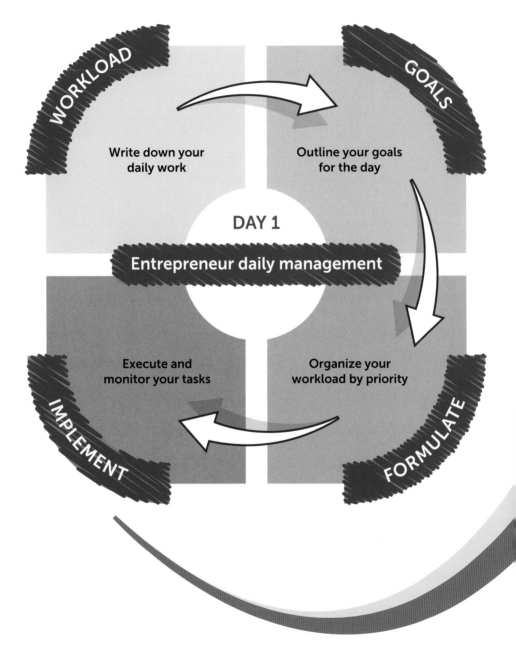

WORKLOAD

GOALS

Write down your daily work

Outline your goals for the day

DAY 1

Entrepreneur daily management

Execute and monitor your tasks

Organize your workload by priority

IMPLEMENT

FORMULATE

If you were asked to climb a large mountain, would you look at it as an impossible task or would you start climbing?

Entrepreneurs take one step at a time and keep moving forward. When they see the size of the mountain ahead of them it does not make them afraid. They understand that it will require effort and sacrifice, and they know that if they keep moving forward, eventually they will reach the top.

The trick to being a successful entrepreneur is to take it one day at a time. Plan what you are going to do each day, every day. Eventually you will complete the work that will help you climb over that mountain.

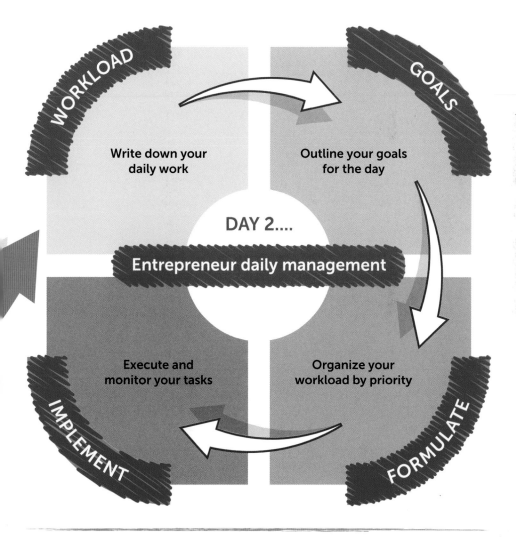

# One Step at a Time

Planning is important, but to be effective it cannot be carried out in a hit-and-miss manner. Successful planning involves following a step-by-step process in each of the various areas of the business.

From the conception of your idea, or vision, to the implementation of your plan, there should be one common factor throughout all phases: you should be following a process that will provide you with a step-by-step guide towards your goal. If you do not follow a process, you will run into problems that you might not even recognize until it is too late. You could end up missing important development steps, failing to identify critical elements that will make or break you, failing to capture all your costs and, overall, reducing your chances for success.

## Following a process will help you focus on what you need to do in an organized approach

The processes commonly used in many organizations deal with management topics, such as communication management, risk management, human resource management, contract management and change management. There are literally hundreds of management processes that can be tailored to your idea, and all it takes is some time on the Internet to find the one you are looking for. There should be absolutely no reason for you to have to rebuild plans or processes. The Internet will provide you with templates you can then adapt to meet your specific needs. If you cannot find the process or the plans you are looking for, keep trying. You might have to combine elements from two or more plans or processes to come up with the right one for you. **So long as you are willing to put the time in, you will always be able to find what you are looking for.** It is never necessary to reinvent the wheel; just apply information that is already there to be accessed. With lessons learned from the experience

Dedication is a must

of other organizations, you will be able to determine, in advance, areas of likely problems and inefficiencies in your operation. The hardest part is knowing where to begin.

I have had many people over the years ask me how I have been able to build my companies without years of experience or education in the fields I was entering. My answer has always been that you don't need to be a subject-matter expert in an industry to be able to build a successful business. All you need to know is how to move a product or service—your idea—through the process. If you have a good idea, before you formalize your business you need to understand the process of how to develop your widget, how to sell your widget, how to market it and how to communicate its value to others. By understanding these as well as many other related matters like human resources, basic finance, risk planning and so forth, you are then able to look at how to employ the right people and the technologies with the capabilities to perform what is required to move your widget business forward.

This is not as easy as it sounds because, as I will discuss in a later section, there are a lot of variables involved in developing an idea and building the business around it. It sometimes feels as though you are going around in circles, but I have found that you succeed better by following processes. The first step is to start defining the plan and start building out more processes as you come across them. Another way to look at a process is as a series of steps or a priority checklist. What do you have to do first? What is next? And so forth.

## MODEL #4

# Entrepreneur Road Map

I can't capture everything that an entrepreneur needs to think about when building their business, however I can provide a little direction. The following details are only a small part of what an entrepreneur will need to know, but this is a good start.

What you should be trying to accomplish as you build out your idea.

When something changes as you build your idea, update what you are trying to accomplish.

High-level tasks that you will need to complete at each stage of the development process.

Change happens and you need to be prepared for it when it does. Learn to adapt as you go.

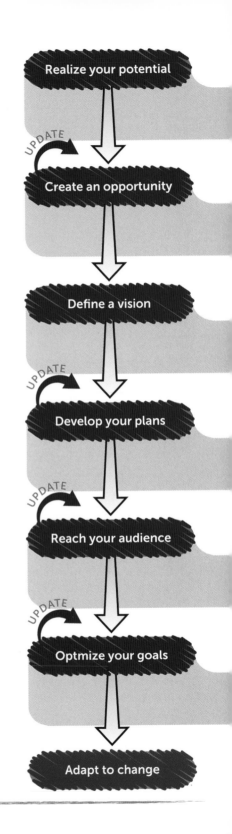

Realize your potential

UPDATE

Create an opportunity

Define a vision

UPDATE

Develop your plans

UPDATE

Reach your audience

UPDATE

Optmize your goals

Adapt to change

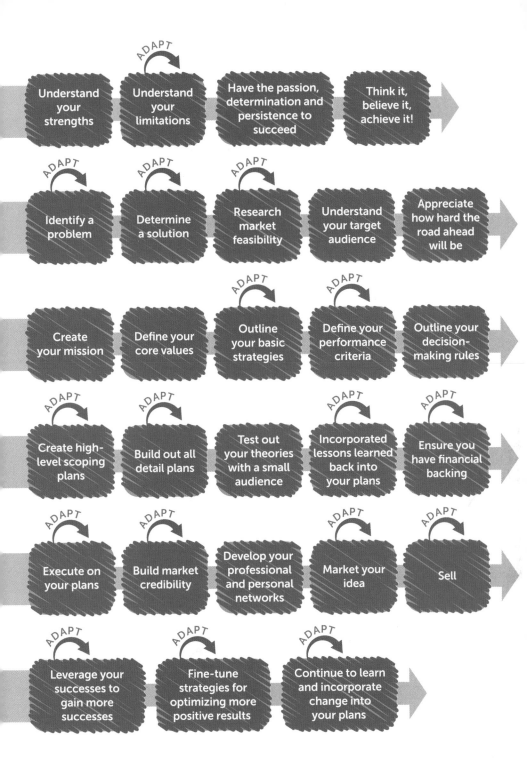

ADAPT
Understand your strengths → Understand your limitations → Have the passion, determination and persistence to succeed → Think it, believe it, achieve it!

ADAPT — Identify a problem → Determine a solution → Research market feasibility → Understand your target audience → Appreciate how hard the road ahead will be

Create your mission → Define your core values → Outline your basic strategies → Define your performance criteria → Outline your decision-making rules

Create high-level scoping plans → Build out all detail plans → Test out your theories with a small audience → Incorporated lessons learned back into your plans → Ensure you have financial backing

Execute on your plans → Build market credibility → Develop your professional and personal networks → Market your idea → Sell

Leverage your successes to gain more successes → Fine-tune strategies for optimizing more positive results → Continue to learn and incorporate change into your plans

# A Picture Is Worth a Thousand Words

Applying the project management technique of defining the "work breakdown structure" is a very effective way of answering the many important questions that need to be asked as you set out to build your business.

It is important at the beginning to ask yourself some basic questions: What needs to be done? Who is going to do it? How are we going to achieve it? When can it reasonably be completed? How much will it cost? What are the main risks involved?

To help come up with useful answers to these kinds of questions, I engage the project management approach of developing a work breakdown structure (WBS). This is a process that involves the breaking down of a project or idea into smaller, manageable components or tasks and listing them all in a sequential format. **In other words, what tasks are required to be completed, in what order, for you to achieve your goal?** The challenge with trying to talk around a WBS structure with potential partners, investors, employees and so forth is that it can sometimes get complicated and unclear, so to help me better explain it, I follow another technique called "modelling." What makes modelling so effective is its ability to show a process as a picture or illustration instead of a series of tasks.

Example WBS

As a visual person, I have found the use of these models to be a very effective means of analyzing and understanding a series of tasks and of answering questions about what needs to be done and how to proceed with doing it. The models I use are illustrations that help me better understand, from the high-level view, the process I need to undertake to achieve my goals both in big-picture planning and for planning the various component pieces. Modelling is also a useful communications tool. I have created hundreds of models over my business career. Because of their visual nature, **I have found many of these make the process of giving reports and presentations more appealing and understandable to different levels of stakeholders.**

Be able to communicate your plan

I am writing another book, *Saving the Words through a Process,* which is intended to show readers how to take an idea and break it down into the individual actions required to implement the idea step by step. I aim to show how these steps can be rolled up into a visual model that makes the process easier to understand. When someone defines their idea in text form only, it can sometimes be hard to follow and can be lost in the words, but when that same idea is laid out as a step-by-step process, it becomes much clearer. I work to simplify the process even further by making a visual model, which is really a picture of what I am trying to build.

The model for your overall plan can be a summary of the main directions and processes envisioned for the development of the business. It shows the combination of all the elements that make up the plan.

These include, but are not limited to

- the mission you want to achieve;
- the business sectors you need to focus on (i.e., business development, operations, sales, marketing);
- your vision for each sector;
- the strategies needed to achieve each vision;
- short-term and long-term objectives and goals;
- a guide to following the project management process (i.e., initiate, plan, execute, control, close);
- a concept starting point.

In order to get to the modelling stage, though, you will need to first work through the details. When I make a presentation to an audience, it is rare that I will include slides that have a lot of text on them. The saying "A picture is worth a thousand words" is very true. I have found that when people include a lot of text in their presentations, it is because they are either not well versed in their topic or nervous that they will forget what to say next. When including a model in your presentations, you are accomplishing

# Saving the words through a process

I have found that the best way to get a message understood is through the use of pictures. You can create pages and pages of descriptive text and risk losing your audience because they either do not have the time to review all the details or they get lost in the words.

When presenting to investors, partners, customers, team members or any other stakeholders, I transform my words first into a process and then into a model. This helps me accomplish further thinking into what I am building, while also providing a means of better explaining to others exactly what I am doing or planning to do.

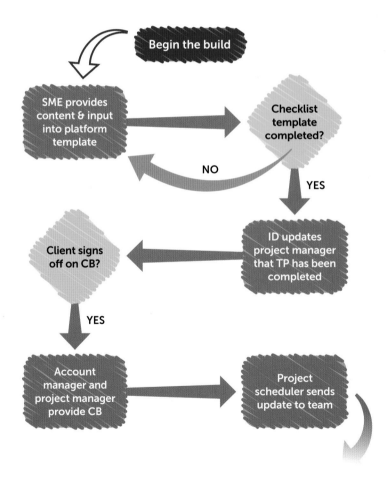

Skillsdox Methodology

Transforming content into mobile results!

Excel · Power Point · Video · Word · DVDs · Audio

CONTENT · CONTEXT · SUBJECT EXPERTS

Podcast · Webcast · Doc. Dowload · PDF Dowload

DEVELOP · DELIVER · APPLY

ASSOCIATION · SKILLSDOX · MEMBERSHIP

PLATFORM

Expert's Video · Need to know · Your notes · Form · Tool kit · Connect · Contact CLE two things: you are providing yourself with a visual reminder of what you should be talking about, while at the same time tapping into more of your audience's cognitive senses. Now they are listening to what you have to say while seeing a visual depiction of the same details. This will help them better remember the message you are working to get across.

# Developing Your Detailed Plan

The step-by-step work required to complete your detailed plan and get it on paper may seem at times tedious, overly detailed and even unnecessary, but it is necessary and will pay big dividends as you put the plan into action.

There is a natural step-by-step course you must take in order to effectively carry out the planning process. It may seem obvious and simple, and perhaps even a bit tedious at times, but it is a necessary process that will bring big rewards.

## Brainstorming

I have found that brainstorming is the best way to empty my head. My mind is constantly working and I have so many thoughts, ideas and concepts running around that I need to get them out in order to focus. Brainstorming is essentially a group activity; the input of others helps to ensure that nothing is missed. At the same time, while I have had many brainstorming sessions with my teams over the years, I have come to realize that I need to brainstorm alone, to get everything out of my head, before I call on others to brainstorm with me. I do this to provide the people with whom I'm brainstorming with a baseline—a place to start out from. When I brainstorm, it is not just a dump of information onto a whiteboard or a piece of paper. I actually follow a process. Here are some examples of some of the things I do.

Brainstorm as many questions as you can think about on what

you want to achieve and write them down. Are there competitors? What is the market like? How do I make a widget? What is the cost of each widget? To whom will I sell my widgets? A few points to keep in mind for brainstorming:

- Write down ideas
- Write down questions
- Gather thoughts
- Anything goes
- Don't put anything in order
- Write down new and old thoughts
- Draw pictures
- Write down risks and issues
- No idea is silly

You will notice that in my brainstorming pictures I write everywhere and have arrows running back and forth to different points or ideas on the board. It may look like a complete mess, but this is because I am working through my thoughts as they come to me. If I already knew the answer, I would just put it down and move on, but the reality is that **most people, if they are like me, need to think and rethink their ideas and what they need to bring them together**.

Brainstorming takes time and focus. Sometimes I leave my "mess" on the whiteboards for days. Then, when I am working on other things, I might glance up at the boards occasionally and add or take away information as I continue to work through the plan.

Keep improving your idea

## Organizing Your Thoughts into a Plan

Once you have put down what you think is everything, you will need to start organizing your thoughts. If you haven't already, you need to put all your thoughts down on paper so that you can revisit them as you move forward with your business development. **Plans change, your direction or concept will change, your thought process may need to be adapted**, but in order to know where you are going, you need to understand where you were. You need to have a baseline plan to build from.

You must be able to make changes

# Write it all down

When building out an idea I brainstorm by asking myself these questions: WHAT, WHO, WHEN, WHERE, HOW and WHY. Each time I add an element under one of these headers, I again ask the same questions about the new element, expanding further and adding in more details under the sections until I can't think of anything else. I also ask WHY for everything I do. When brainstorming, there are both inputs and outputs that need to be considered for both inside and outside your control. If you look at WHO as the component you are brainstorming around, you must consider the other components like WHAT, HOW, WHEN & WHERE as an input. In order for you to know the size of your team for example, you will first need to know WHAT you are building, HOW it will be built and WHEN it will need to be completed. If you are building something complicated, you would probably need more team members or partners than you would if the idea was simple.

*Simply change the title from "promote a widget" to whatever you want to brainstorm and follow the same approach.*

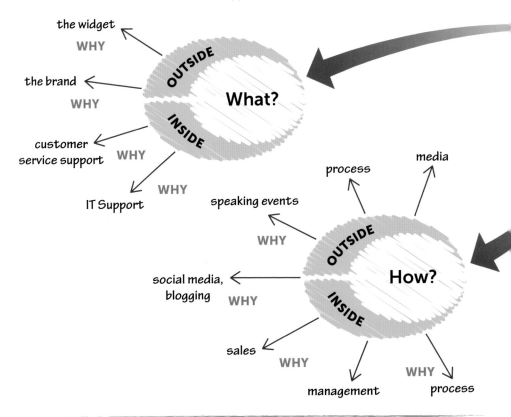

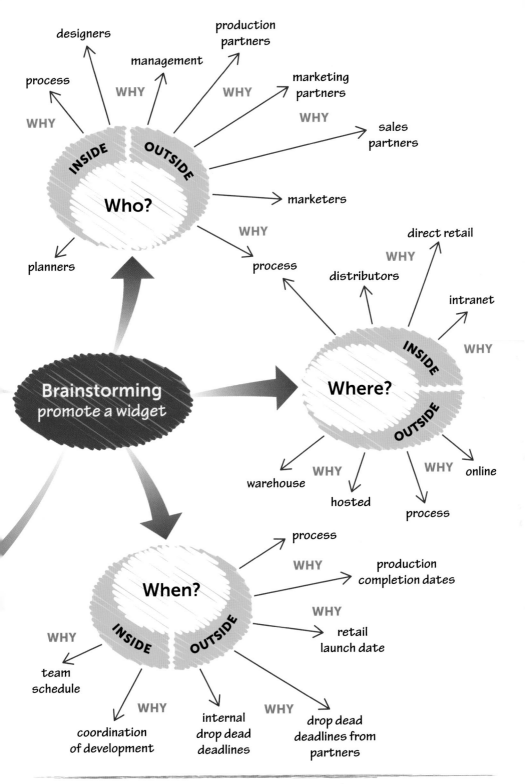

As you proceed, you may need to create other plans as well, but they will be natural outputs from your work breakdown structure and main business plan. This book will not get into details about building business plans; there are many books that provide blueprints for what you need, and even step-by-step guides. The following are examples of plans you may need to develop as you continue down the planning path and gain a better understanding of your requirements: production plan, human resources plan, risk plan, quality control plan, budget, procurement plan, integration plan, strategies, scope change plan and time management plan. There are, of course, many different plans that could apply to you, depending on the nature of your business.

The business plan is a summary of the past, present and future for your business, all put together into one document.

From the past, you need to understand the answers to questions like

- What has worked?
- What has failed?
- What similar products have previously existed?
- What are your previous experiences?

Experiences do not necessarily have to come from running your own business. When I first started, I had no experience in business and had to use what I could.

From the present, you need to understand things like

- today's marketplace;
- your target customer;
- regulations that might apply to your idea;
- purchasing sensitivities such as price and placement;
- environmental impacts caused by your product;
- the resources needed in order to meet the future;
- the problem your product/service is solving.

For the future, you need to understand things like

- your visions;
- your missions;
- your objectives;
- your strategies to achieve the above;
- risk assessments on things that might go wrong or present big challenges.

## Using Planning Templates

It may appear at this point that your planning is completed, but planning should continue. You need to keep working through what is required to understand your past, present and future. The best way to make your continuing planning simpler is through the use of templates. A template is a document framework that has already been developed and used by many others as a guide to developing their detailed documents. There are templates for every plan you can imagine; you just need to track them down. Templates should be used whenever you need to start building something. But remember, a template is not a plan.

## Using Your Plans to Sell Your Idea

**The one thing that people, whether they be investors, partners or potential clients, will want to see more than anything else, if they are going to take your idea seriously, is your plans.** They need to know if you've thought through what you intend on developing—the costs, the risks, the opportunities, the requirements, the constraints, the way you intend to handle all challenges, and the return you expect to provide your future stakeholders. Your plans should provide answers and reassurance on all these items and much more.

Your plans

# 4

# The Power of of Leverage

# Leverage: A Key Element

> The power of leverage means taking advantages, or apparent disadvantages, and turning them into something that will help us get what we want or need. Leverage is a capability we all have within us if we choose to exploit it.

Just as project management has been the key to my business planning, discovering and using the power of leverage has been the key to my ability to get the most out of whatever resources, however meagre, I have had at a given time. Leveraging is using your advantages, or sometimes your apparent disadvantages, to get something you want or need in order to move ahead.

The first time I really learned about the power of leverage was when I was 13 years old. During summer vacation, my brothers and I decided to have a yard sale with all those toys we had found in the dumpster earlier. We had spent a good part of the winter fixing whatever toys we could. We spread hundreds of them across several large tables we had pulled out from our basement and a few blankets we had stretched out across the grass. Our neighbourhood was always filled with kids like us, so we had a large number of potential customers. All we had to do was sell the toys for $1 to $5 each and we would have a ton of money. In one afternoon, my brothers and I made more than $300. To a 13-year-old, that is a lot of money. Because it was almost as much as our monthly welfare cheques, our parents took the money to hold for us; they gave it back to us bit by bit as we needed it, but it soon vanished. From the experience, I learned about negotiating and how to read people in order to get what I wanted—valuable lessons in leveraging and credibility-building that later helped me develop many small companies, which slowly grew into bigger ones, and eventually into my first multimillion-dollar company. I also learned that even though we had earned that money, it still didn't really belong to us.

People have asked me, over the years, how I was able to leverage so much when I had so little, and I've always found it hard to explain because it just came naturally to me. If you spend enough time working on something—some observers have estimated that it takes about 10,000 hours—eventually you become an expert at it. When I was very young, all my energy was focused on struggling, problem-solving and learning to leverage. I had surpassed the 10,000-hour point in practising all those skills before I was in my late teens.

## Determining what you are naturally good at could provide you with your baseline of skills that can be leveraged

I came up with this analogy to help illustrate how being put into a different situation can force you to learn how to leverage. Imagine you wake up in the middle of a thick forest, thousands of miles from civilization. In your pocket, you find a note that says you must survive on your own in the wilderness for six months with neither food nor shelter, with none of the conveniences you have relied on at home, and with no one to call upon for help. What do you do? You need to survive. You may feel helpless for a while, but eventually you'll draw on your survival instincts to leverage whatever things are available to you in the forest to make it through. In the world of business, as in that forest, we all have resources to draw on for survival and to move ahead when we absolutely need them. **We only need to understand how to use those resources to our advantage and turn problems into solutions.** There is a cure for cancer; we just haven't found it yet. There is a way to travel across the universe; we just haven't discovered it yet. The possibilities are there, and we need only get past our perceived limitations in order to achieve them.

Be able to leverage your skills

Over the years, I have learned that in order to leverage something you need or want it is helpful to understand the other party's (the leveragee's) points of interest. What makes them tick? What turns them away? What are their pain areas? Knowing the answers to these questions will help you plan your approach. In advertising, the most important step is getting to know your audience, and the same applies here. It's difficult to sell something if you don't understand the other parties' likes and dislikes, and most important, what you can do or say to make them want to help you. The following are examples of some points-of-interest questions you should be able to answer prior to engaging with the other person:

- What are their concerns?
- What are their limitations?
- Do they have to get approval to do a deal with you?
- What are they most afraid of?
- Do they have financial obligations to meet?
- How do they get personally compensated?
- Do they have exclusive contracts?
- Do they like their current partners?
- What do they like to do in their free time?
- Do they have a budget?
- Do they have a purchasing timeline?
- Are they bound by a union?
- What do they like to do on their own time?

Once you have determined their points of interest, you can start to plan how you will engage them. Here are a few examples:

- Engage them with details about other opportunities you are involved in that tie into their points of interest.
- Let them know you have credibility in the field.
- Be present and in their line of sight often.
- Ensure that you update, on a regular basis, all key contacts on the progress of your business and objectives.
- Meet in person when you can to build up personal relationships.
- Network as often as you can with as many people as you can.
- Present your material in a professional manner.
- Live up to your promises and obligations.

# Everything Is Leverageable

The power of leverage is your ability to make things happen or to change an outcome in your favour. It is a way of convincing others that you have something they need, a solution to their problem. The solution could be anything: a product, service, idea, relationship, lesson learned or situation.

In a sense, the use of leverage is a barter system that taps into your creative process and guides others to their desired outcomes while you, at the same time, are achieving your own. I call it a barter system because, typically, when we first start developing a business, we don't have money to pay for the things we need or want, so we must barter to get them. The more you are able to put into the process, the more you will receive from it. It's not about manipulation, trickery or lying, but simply showing people that they need you as much as you need them, and that finding a solution together will be a win-win for everyone involved. Almost anything can be leveraged.

## Success

It is generally accepted that success breeds success. If you are successful, people like to know what you are doing to achieve that success, and they want to participate. When I sold my second business, I was at dinner with a colleague, Adrian, whom I had known for years. He asked me when I was going to build my next business—he was willing to invest in it. **I didn't even have a business at the time, but here was someone willing to invest** in one with me. I had proven that I was able to build businesses that work. On the strength of that, he was willing to support me without even knowing what any new business might look like.

Credibility adds future value

## Failure

It may not be obvious how failure can be leveraged to your advantage in business. The key is to be able to show that you have learned from your mistakes and that you are able to move forward more productively. Sometimes, people make many of the same mistakes over and over again and, for some reason, still think the outcome will be different next time. Learning from mistakes and not repeating them can turn failure into a powerful leveraging agent for success. It is at the point of failure that one's will to continue and mount a comeback is truly tested. Failure also provides an educational experience; unless you have gone through it, you never really know how you will behave when you're at your lowest point in business.

## Imagination

Having a great imagination provides you with the ability to show people your vision and get them to really buy into it. Telling a story around your idea is Sales 101, but being creative and leveraging your imagination can take people deep into your thinking so that they truly understand what you are trying to accomplish. Business plans, with their facts, figures and summaries, are okay to a point, but the *story* of the business idea can be much more effective in helping someone truly understand where you want to take the business.

## Sales

One of the best things you can have going for you when you are looking for money to develop your business is sales or purchase orders for sales. You hear it all the time on TV shows like *Dragon's Den* or *Shark Tank,* which put entrepreneurs in front of seasoned investors and successful businesspeople. The entrepreneurs make a pitch for investment money from one or more of the investors, based on their great business idea and their ability to make the investors more money. One of the most common questions the investors ask is "What sales do you have?" For most of the entrepreneurs, this is their doom. They do not have sales, which indicates: (1) that no one is interested in the product or service, or (2) that the entrepreneur does not know how to sell effectively. The reality is, without sales or purchase orders, you are lacking a valuable leverage item.

## Possibility

Sometimes, the possibility of another opportunity in business can be as valuable as an actual purchase order or a closed deal. When I connect with someone on an opportunity, I often refer to another opportunity or other projects I might be working on in the future. Knowing that I am in discussions with a potential competitor, or another company with established credibility, the other party automatically sees me as someone with business credibility. When I speak with investors, I bring up these possibilities, mentioning people I've spoken to and what they've said. I even go so far as showing email communications I have had with someone else to demonstrate that I really have been in such discussions. Whether or not the opportunity ever comes to fruition isn't relevant in that context. Rather, the possibility that something *might* occur is enough to create the setting I need. The potential is a driving factor that can help you when you need to turn your possibilities into results.

## Fear

It is amazing to see how people react when they realize that their competitors might be working with you. During meetings, I would sometimes leave my notebook open to a page containing details about a competitor. From time to time, the person I was meeting with would glance more and more inquisitively at my notes. Something had caught their eye: "... closing a deal with ABC company in 2 weeks." I have used this approach many times during meetings. I would open emails to show examples of work and, in the process, scroll past a folder with their competitor's name on it. Most people would automatically stop me and ask what we were doing for that company, providing me an opening to leverage a possibility. Now they would be fearful that their competitor might be one step ahead of them. By leveraging their concern over that possibility, I increased their interest in my products. I would not be misleading them, because I would only talk about what we were planning or discussing with the competitor. I would not get into too much detail about any conversations I'd had—these would be confidential—just enough for them to see that there were possibilities. I would never lie to a buyer, but I don't mind letting them come to their own conclusions.

## Professionalism

Sometimes, doing little things can make a big difference in business. Being early to meetings, sending thank-you notes right after a meeting, following up right away on discussion points, being prompt, polite, courteous and helpful whenever you can . . . these are some ways you can leverage professionalism. These small gestures, of course, are also part of great customer service. When I work with people, I try my best not to put the sale before the customer. The sale will come, but the relationship needs to be built, and a professional approach in your business dealings will certainly help in doing that.

## Knowledge

Being prepared for a client meeting is critically important; anticipating all the questions that might be asked is even more important. Leveraging knowledge and being able to effectively answer questions even before they are asked is impressive in a client setting. When I was building my business, I noticed that the same types of questions were being asked in meetings, so I adjusted my presentations to incorporate those questions as well as answers to them. As more questions would surface, I would repeat the process until I had identified all the questions and thought through the answers in advance. I have attended many meetings where, at the end, the buyers would say, "I actually have no questions. I had a list of questions to ask, but you answered them one after another." This would not only impress them, but also show that I knew what I was doing.

## Strength

By strength, in this context, I mean a combination of confidence and passion in your presentations and discussions that allows you to stand up to challenges and be convincing in your arguments. When I was younger, I didn't have this inner strength. As I developed it over the years and leveraged it in presentations at meetings or to larger groups, it led people to trust in my insights and arguments, and they would often remark on how much I loved my work.

## Passion

Showing people that you really believe in what you are selling requires more than telling them that you really believe in it. You must let them see it for themselves. When you are really passionate about something, it comes out in your excitement, how you hold yourself and talk with confidence. This is another powerful trait that you can leverage. If others see how passionate you are about what you are doing, you gain their confidence because they can feel that you will do whatever it takes to be successful.

## Courage

No matter what other traits you may have to leverage, if you do not have the courage to do it, you will not succeed. Courage may not come easily; sometimes you need to dig deep to find it. But leveraging your courage will bring you to places you never thought could be possible. Cold calling, working trade shows, speaking at conferences, presenting your ideas, leading meetings, managing team members and conducting negotiations all require your ability to leverage your courage.

### Taking the time to understand what you have to leverage will help you better plan out how and when to leverage it

A good example of the kind of positive results that leveraging these last three traits (strength, passion and courage) can bring is a speaking engagement I had at the Canadian Society of Training and Development Conference in November 2010. I was about to speak to more than 150 people about how I thought e-learning should be developed and how, in my view, the current approach to it was incorrect. Leading up to the speech, I was extremely nervous because, compared with my audience of PhDs, instructional designers and educational types who had been practising in the learning field for much longer than I had been in the business world altogether, I was quite new. However, I fought my anxiety and, during my presentation, projected a high level of confidence and inner strength and spoke very passionately on my subject. The result was a standing ovation and a swarm of people rushing to the front to get my business card. My business partner, who was videotaping the presentation from the back of the room, was in awe. He could not believe the response I had elicited. To be honest, neither could I. It was a pleasant surprise—a result of leveraging my strengths to make a case for a new idea in the e-learning field.

## Money

It goes without saying that having money is critical in business, but sometimes, cultivating the impression that you have cash available can also be critical. When you work with banks, lenders, suppliers and even customers, cash in the bank is the most leverageable thing you can have, but most start-ups usually have very little. The second-best asset you can have is purchase orders. Even though you might not have cash available to you, if you can drum up a lot of sales orders, people will see the value in what you are doing and start to invest in it. From a development perspective, most people say you need capital up front in order to go get sales, but a true entrepreneur can acquire sales without products. In my first company, I started off with letter-sized paper that I folded and glued together to make tiny boxes. I brought these to my very first client, Bill Wyman, the president of Hallmark's Ottawa franchises, and asked him to envision what they would look like to scale. Armed only with my paper boxes, some limited sales materials that contained pricing and other information about the company, which had been printed off my $125 inkjet printer, along with my passion, the possibilities and my professionalism, I landed a $1,200 order. With this leveraging of very limited financial resources, I was able to start a business that five years later was doing more than $4 million in revenue.

## Contacts

Developing good business relationships is one of the essential requirements for growing a business. It is required not only in order for you to build your own network, but also as a way of building your credibility. Your contacts or contact list can be leveraged in a manner that shows you are "out there." This will provide you with a level of credibility that can work to your advantage. Building contacts can happen anywhere. Whether at meetings or on the golf course with businesspeople I don't yet know, I ask a lot of questions in order to become better acquainted with them personally. These questions, and the conversations they lead to, usually open the door to other connections as you discover you have mutual relationships. In some regards, the world can be seen as a small place; the more you network, the smaller you make it.

## Family

Family can be an effective leveraging opportunity simply because they are family and are willing to help. I may not have had much in the way of family connections to leverage, but when I knew that my now-mother-in-law worked at the Bank of Canada, I thought about how I could leverage that relationship to get myself in the door. I had many family members willing to help me whenever they could as I built my business; they worked on the assembly line, helped to develop marketing materials or product designs, and even attended meetings with me. Leveraging family is easy in some ways, but more complicated in others, as I'll discuss later.

## Time

By leveraging time, I mean taking advantage of whatever time you can to do more than someone else might do. For example, most people work nine to five, come home and make dinner, sit on the couch, watch TV or hang out in their back yard. After work is done, they are done with work. To succeed and advance yourself further, you have to work harder and smarter. While you are sitting on the couch watching TV, for example, what if, at the same time, you did a little extra work on your business idea. If you did this each night for a week, you would be gaining several productive hours while still relaxing, without any real stress or hardship, and making more progress on building your future. I have heard people say so often that they just don't have enough time, but in reality, we all have the same amount of time. Our days, weeks and months are all precisely the same. It is how we choose to use that time that makes the difference.

## Credibility

Building credibility is also crucial to successfully developing and maintaining a business. It is one of the most important things you have to leverage, and it supports all your other leveraging efforts. Having credibility means people trust you and see you as a caring, supportive leader. Leveraging credibility involves using that trust, which you have built up over time, to bring more credibility and success. You build credibility by showing people that you are capable of achieving success. With customers, this could entail showing them other people's work and getting good references. With employees, leading by example and providing a workplace that promotes personal growth and satisfaction will be effective. With suppliers, being able to pay your bills and communicate effectively, if there are any issues, will build credibility. Of course, you can always tap into other resources to gain credibility in your industry. Generating white papers, writing articles and speaking at events can be useful ways of introducing yourself, your concepts and your business to your peers. Not only that, but they are free advertising!

# Leveraging for Revenue and Value

When using the power of leverage, you're not only focusing on money, you're also investing in the long-term value of your company. Non-monetary value in a business is intangible, but it can, over the long run, bring significant tangible benefits.

Not everyone sees value as a second stream in business. If you look only at what is in front of you, you will overlook it, but when you look deeper into your overall vision, you will see that not just revenue but value, too, is important. Both in planning your business and building it, you need to include both streams.

When I started iPal Interactive Learning, my business partner, Scott Hunter, did not like the fact that I wasn't only focused on driving revenues but was also working to build future value. Since we were a start-up, he wanted me to concentrate on getting the deals closed first and worry about building value later. We needed revenue sooner rather than later, for sure, so as usual, he had a point, but only a partial one. One of the first things they teach you in business school is that cash is king. If you don't have cash flow to support your operations, pay your bills, keep your people employed and grow your business, you won't be in business for long. So, undoubtedly, revenue is critical to the success of any business, but I think there **needs to be a balance between driving revenue and creating value in order to build a solid foundation for your business**. Without value, you're not creating *future* worth. Driving revenue will pay the bills, but it will not necessarily set you up for the long term. In

Build future value

one of my previous businesses, I did not create the value I needed from the beginning. As a result, I was always chasing revenue to pay for current operations. If I had focused on both immediate revenues and value at the same time, eventually the value would have provided me with the long-term revenue stream I needed.

## Without value, you're not creating future worth. Focus on both immediate revenue and value.

When I think about creating value, I think of the movie *The Godfather*. In the movie, the Mafia is always willing to offer help and favours to other people; later, they collect on those favours to create future value in their organization. They give a little bit of what they have so that they can get what they really want. It may seem like an extreme example (and I'm not saying you should send someone to sleep with the fishes to get what you want), but basically my approach is similar. If you are willing to create value for someone else by giving them something you have, there's a good chance that person will feel they owe you something in return. It's just human nature, and there's nothing wrong with using it to your advantage to create value.

Although value is immeasurable, it can contribute to significant concrete positive results. On the other hand, its absence can weaken a business.

# Building tomorrow, today

Generating sales is absolutely critical, but focusing only on today's revenue could be harmful to your future success as you grow.

When building today, you must also consider what you need to do in order to build for the future as well. This is not as easy as I make it sound because you have to spend time on projects that do not help pay the bills today.

Picture this: You do not have any money and you don't have a home to live in. Your first priority would probably be to gather food and then seek shelter. You can do this every day and would probably be successful at it, but for how long? What if, instead, each day you also looked for a large stone that you could start to build your own house, one brick at a time! At first, this might seem like a waste of effort, but over time the foundation would eventually start to come together, followed by the walls and then a roof. Now instead of having to find food and shelter, you would only need to find food as you would now have a home. This would now enable you to focus on building a garden to be able to supply your future food supply.

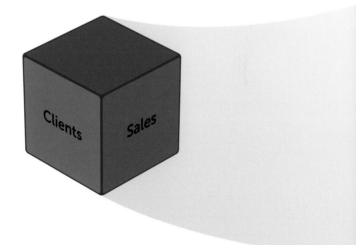

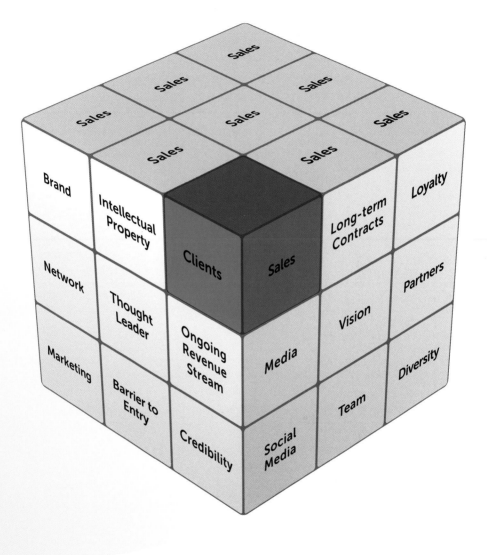

If you want to ensure that you're creating value in your business, it's important to have diversity in contracts and to make them long-term. This is a lesson I wish I had learned earlier in my career. When I did realize it, in order to help create long-term value, I started to focus on longer-term contracts with distributors, customers, and so forth.

Signing short-term contracts was one of the biggest mistakes I made when developing my first business. When I worked with Disney, our contracts were for only one to three years, with no guarantee of an automatic renewal. Potential acquirers pointed this out as a negative. They indicated that if our contracts were not renewed, we would lose a lot of the value our company had built up. When companies were thinking about purchasing EasyWrapLines, they looked for added value in several key areas:

- long-term contracts that provided us with benefit and flexibility;
- diversity in contracts, customers and partners;
- repeating revenue stream;
- intellectual property;
- profitability;
- wide distribution network.

I had contracts, but with only a few customers, and as a result I was at risk of being forced to close my company if we lost one or two of the deals. My production partners were also few in number. I did not own my distribution channels, which meant that I did not have control over the end-user of our products. The intellectual property (IP) that I had belonged to Disney and the other entertainment companies. The key to creating value is to ensure that if you lose a few partners or customers, your business will not fall apart. Long-term contracts with a diversity of companies will help ensure that. Partners and clients may ask you for exclusivity. The best advice I can provide is, if they want exclusivity, you need to ask what they are willing to give in return. It has to be a win-win arrangement; otherwise you will likely pay the price later, and that price could even be your business.

Long-term contracts are valuable but, when negotiating them, you need to build in enough flexibility to ensure that you are not hindered down the road by too many restrictions. With my current business, I've learned my lesson. I already have a lot of value drivers in place, such as long-term contracts across numerous and diverse industries, partners and customers, IP that belongs to iPal, and a continuous revenue stream.

# Leveraging Nothing to Get Something

When you think you have absolutely nothing to leverage, it is time to think harder and get creative. You could actually have more than you first realize.

The power of leverage is often about finding treasures among the trash, seeing them for what they are and using them to your advantage. I would never have been successful in business if I hadn't leveraged what little I had at the beginning to get what I needed to move ahead.

The early stages of business development are the most challenging; you have no references and no credibility that you can leverage in order to grow. As a new entrepreneur, I was competing with industry giants like Hallmark and American Greetings. How could I compete with such big companies, with all their resources, their well-established customers and distribution networks? If I wanted to convince customers to buy my product lines, I had to get creative. The art of selling is the ability to convince the other person, in a way that best suits their needs, that you have something they need. You have to address their concerns, which in my business are usually around cost and credibility. To gauge your credibility, most customers and suppliers will look at factors such as what you've done, whom you've worked with and who's on your team. These assets aren't developed overnight, and so, in order to gain credibility, I decided to leverage one customer with another.

For example, I was trying to sell my products to Dollar General, one of the largest American dollar store chains. I needed to let them know that I was in discussions with other dollar stores in order to make them worried (just a little bit) about what their competitors were doing. I had to be subtle about it, though, because I didn't want them to feel manipulated or threatened. I couldn't just say, "Well, if you don't buy from us, Family Dollar [their direct competitor] will have a major advantage over you." Instead, at just the right moment, I would slip in something like, "That's a very good point. Family Dollar mentioned that as well." That technique almost always piqued their interest. I like to call this technique "planting the seed."

## "Planting the seed" helps direct a conversation to achieve your objective while making it seem like it was their idea

Leveraging fear, as described earlier, would not only get them thinking but also make them believe I was bigger than I really was, which made me seem more reputable. When they started to ask me more questions, they felt as though they were the ones opening the door for discussion, when in fact I was the one who had planted the seed. I may not always have closed the deal with these customers, but the more I was able to get them into discussions with me, the more I could leverage those discussions in order to gain more credibility and market interest.

Planting the seed can be difficult. It requires forethought to make sure you are not being obvious about it. I first think about what I want the outcome of a meeting to be, and then about how to start a conversation that will lead another person in the direction that will likely bring the result I want. You have to be subtle and you need to understand the person you are talking with so that you know how to position the conversation. In order to plant these seeds, do your research first on what you want, **who your target is and what you think they would want. Understanding their pain areas and/or their point-of-interest areas** will help you position your conversation to address either one or both.

Leverage point-of-interest areas

I used the same technique when trying to obtain production partners. I would meet with multiple suppliers and talk to them about prospective customers, the size of the potential production runs, and other suppliers' terms and conditions. I had to paint a picture of how big the opportunity could get, and they had to understand where they fit into that picture. How were they going to make money? What did a future with my company look like? All they needed was a reason to support my company in making product, and I was determined to give them several reasons.

Planting the seed is probably one of my favourite techniques for getting what I want. I have leveraged my persuasive skills to lead people down a winding path that might not have been obvious to them at that time and usually took months to complete, but in the end I would get what I wanted without them suspecting they were being led to that outcome. It works more often than not.

A great example is when I wanted to increase our licence rights with all licensors to include other territories outside Canada. After I had been awarded contract rights for a product line in Canada, I would then try to get the rights to the same products in other countries. This would be done by leveraging our production and distribution model. The opportunity was that I could leverage our production runs that were being produced overseas in mass quantities and than simply ship to multiple destinations around the world. This would enable us to produce in larger runs, reducing our cost per unit and enabling us to sell products seamlessly around the world. Each country would benefit from the creativeness and uniqueness of our product lines.

Disney liked this idea, and so did many other licensors, but their main challenge was that they already had partners with rights in those territories, so they had to pass on our opportunity. This did not deter me from my goal. What I got from their rejection was that they needed the ability to justify that there were going to be significant orders through us for our products that their other partners could not provide. I knew what I had to do: I had to convince large retailers from around the world to give me orders for a product I did not have the rights to sell.

Over a period of months, when I met with retailers from around the world, I would plant the seed about how well our licensed products were selling in Canada and would then proceed to open our catalogue up to the page where there were designs for the product lines we had rights to in their country. In some cases, I might only have one product for their country. I never once told them we could sell them products we did not have rights to. What was important was for them to see me flipping through all the other lines we carried. When I landed on the page that had what was available for them, they all would react the same way: "That is it? I want the other stuff."

This provided the opening I was looking for. I would explain that we did not have the rights in their territory and that, if the retailer was really interested in getting our products, I would have to convince the licensors to give them to us. I would, of course, also mention that it would have to be a really compelling story for them to agree. In the end, I had many retailers contacting our licensors and, in some cases, providing me with multimillion orders if the licensor would give us the rights.

# Juggling on the Run

It is part of an entrepreneur's life to be able to juggle many tasks, and you should be prepared not only for tasks you didn't identify, but also picking up others that you did not expect you'd have to do. Juggling the many elements involved in growing your business is especially challenging in the early stages.

Working to raise money to get your business growing would not be as big a challenge if you could devote all your time and energy to that task alone. The reality is, trying to raise funds for the business is but one of several important jobs you have to focus on, all at the same time. This is what I call the "circular development problem": the need to accomplish one thing that can't be done unless something else is completed first, but that second item can't be completed before a third is done, and so on. All the tasks need to be completed simultaneously because each depends on the successful completion of the others.

# MODEL #8
# Circular Development Problem

Multi-tasking is a strength that an entrepreneur will need to have, especially when building a business up from an idea. If all you have is an idea, you need to think through how to get the idea off the ground. In this example, there are three main hubs: Money, Product and Client. Between each hub there are example items that you might need in order to move from hub to hub. The challenge that most entrepreneurs face is moving between hubs, because they don't have one or more of the items that they need to be able to move forward. The Circular Development Problem means that in order for an entrepreneur to move forward they must leverage one or more of the elements between the hubs. For example: A purchase order could be used to leverage credibility to get an investment that would be used to pay for production and delivery.

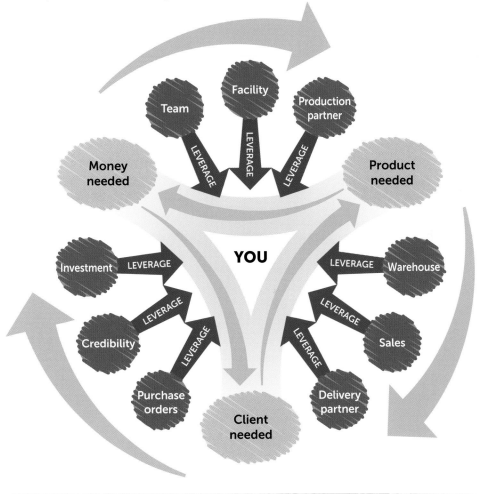

In building my business I found that, without money, it was hard to travel to meet with prospective customers. Without customers, I couldn't get orders, and without orders, I couldn't get banks or investors to finance me. With no financing, I couldn't develop products. With no products, I had nothing to sell and no credibility. Without credibility, I had no opportunities to develop partnerships in manufacturing, distribution and sales, and no opportunities meant no money. No money meant it was hard to meet prospective customers. And the wheel goes round and round.

There are, of course, some aspects of developing your business that you can work on with some degree of isolation from the others. You can start your business plan, for example, from the beginning and work your way through. But when it comes to putting that plan into action, you will have multiple things happening all at once. One important key to working your way through this challenging growing period lies in the plan itself. As I've detailed in Chapter 3, you need to identify all of your tasks and put them in order. You will see that, when broken down into smaller steps, the big jobs reveal some tasks that follow one another in a logical sequence and some that, more or less, must be done at the same time. The latter will require a bit of creativity and skill to address.

## Multi-tasking is more than just managing many tasks—it is about adapting each task to change as you move your idea forward

As I suspect is the case with all successful entrepreneurs, my solution was to learn to juggle several tasks at once by leveraging one group of tasks against another. This took a lot of time, it didn't come easy and I made a lot of mistakes. But perhaps because I like juggling and can do a decent job of juggling three balls (including throwing them under my leg and around my back), I was able to learn how to juggle business tasks as well. The trick is to work at two or more items at the same time, leveraging one to achieve results with another so that, bit by bit, people see your progress and become more willing to support you.

The following are some examples of how I have exploited this strategy:

## Getting a customer

In order to get my first customer who would agree to put my products in their stores, I had to find someone willing to purchase the products based only on visual aids rather than the actual items. Because I did not have the funds to pay for production, I had no real products to demonstrate. To get around this, I would create mock-up samples of my products and printouts of marketing materials to use in meetings with potential customers. I was completely honest with them: I let them know that I needed someone to take a chance on my product. To persuade them to do this, I would give them a great deal on price, in some cases even offering the product for free. **When I got a customer, I would leverage that one to get another, using this first customer as a reference.** Then I would leverage the first and the second to get a third, and so on. Leveraging your success with other customers, even if they include one who is not paying for your product or service, is important

Leverage customers

because it shows that there is interest in what you're selling. It is also important to secure more customers to flow your product through in case the product doesn't sell with the initial ones. The key to making all this work is finding a way to get someone willing to take a chance on you. If you can mitigate their risks, they will be more than willing to give you a try.

## Getting a production partner

Once you have a customer or two who is willing to support you, you can use this information to help find a production partner. Just as with trying to get customers, you leverage opportunity against success. My approach was to meet with many local production plants to show them what I was building. I would walk them through the opportunity and ask if they were willing to work with me on developing the products. I would leverage the customer who had agreed to take on my product line and then try to sell the plant on giving me credit terms for the production run.

Most did not want to do this, but I eventually found a couple that did because **they liked the opportunity and liked the fact that I had a customer interested in taking on the line**.

## Getting investors

**Leverage clients for production** With a couple of customers and production partners lined up, the next trick was to convince someone to give me money to pay for the production once its payment due-date arrived. Since I was getting credit terms, I would still be required to pay for the product, even if it did not sell in my customers' stores. This is often the most difficult leveraging element, because you need to convince someone to give up real money to support what you are doing without the kind of proven success they like to see.

Investors want to see information about your actual sales, resources, customers, prospects, partners, market conditions and your own problem-solving skills. For investors, it is all about their risk exposure. If you have lots of sales, continuous revenue streams and a clear indication of how they can make money, investing is an easier prospect. However, if you are just trying to build sales and do not have a proven track record, their risks are higher and they are much less willing to part with their money. The trick here is to leverage the fact that you have customers and production people coming on board and that all the pieces are coming together. If you can convince them that you are on the path to success, that you have the necessary perseverance and understanding to achieve that success, and that you have your own money on the line, they may be more open to the idea of investing in your enterprise. Unfortunately, I could not get any big investors to give me the money I needed when I started. I had to go to family and friends, looking for smaller amounts, instead.

I continued to juggle the various elements of normal operational tasks: looking after customers, keeping track of production, making sales pitches and garnering small investments from family and friends, leveraging whatever limited successes I was achieving along the way. Even after the products started to sell, I still had very little cash flow. I had to go back to the people at the production plant and persuade them to turn out more products on terms, even though the first order had still not been paid for. As the plant's risks increased with this extended credit, their willingness to continue to back me started to waver. This is when the investors started to play an even more important role, by providing money for production as well as additional sales initiatives. **Fortunately, by leveraging my modest successes, I was gradually able to get some bigger investors on board.**

Leverage success for investment

# Growing Pains

AS YOU ARE STARTING YOUR BUSINESS AND WORKing through the early phases to develop it, you will face numerous challenges. Some of these will be minor and temporary, but others will be much bigger and more persistent. The latter will likely have to do, in one way or another, with issues of time, money and stress. How you deal with these growing pains, and in particular how well you perform in the face of challenges and how creative you are at addressing them, will be the true test of your entrepreneurial mettle.

# Bumps and Bruises

As part of the growing pains of building a business, you will experience many bumps and bruises along the way. The trick is to pick yourself up, learn from the experience and move forward again.

I sometimes compare the challenges new entrepreneurs face as they struggle to get their business off the ground to the bumps and bruises a child takes while learning to ride a bike.

When my son, Eric, was seven years old, we decided it was time for the training wheels to come off his bike. He was reaching a major milestone in his childhood, and like most life changes, the biggest thing holding him back was fear. He was afraid of hurting himself, afraid of failing and afraid of disappointing me. The first ride without training wheels started out well enough. My wife and daughters and several neighbours were all standing around watching as he moved forward—first slowly, and then faster, with me jogging alongside, helping to keep him balanced. He felt he was doing great, and so he asked me to let go. I did, and a few seconds later I was picking him up from the pavement, wiping the tears from his face and the blood from his legs.

After some bandaging and hugs inside, we went back out to try again. But this time, the nature of the battle had changed. Now, instead of just teaching him to ride a bike, I had to teach him self-confidence as well, a tougher challenge. After a few more falls,

# Don't be afraid to fail

When faced with a challenge, do you think you can move forward? I created this process to help you understand your choice of either "YES, MAYBE or NO" could result in a positive or negative outcome. Where do you land most of the time?

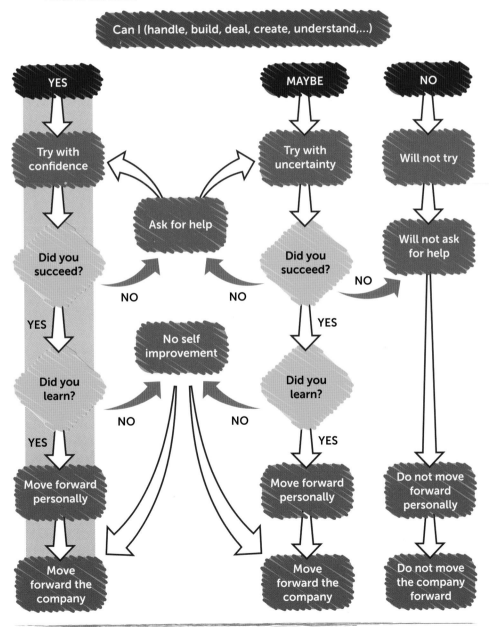

that old destroyer of dreams, fear, was getting to him and he was beginning to say, "I can't." To help ease his fears, I equipped him with several pieces of sports padding—shin pads, knee pads and elbow pads—and now that he felt less pain, his self-confidence soon took off. Two hours later he could go 50 feet, and in a few days he could ride entirely on his own without falling.

As an entrepreneur, you will encounter many falls and experience many bumps and bruises as you struggle with the growing pains of building your businesses. **The trick is to brush yourself off and get back up on the bike, hopefully having learned from the experience and gained in confidence.**

Don't give up

# Digging for Dollars

When working to raise money, you can't assume it will just be handed to you. You need to know everything about your business, your industry and your competitors. You should have plans to show where you intend to go and how you will get there, including how your idea will produce revenue. Above all, you need to be persistent and careful.

Regardless of how much you sacrifice in the early stages in order to save money, as a beginning entrepreneur you will most likely not have enough of your own to develop your business. You will most likely have to depend on other sources to keep going. You can look for help from banks, government organizations or private investors, but they often impose a lot of restrictions and requirements that people just starting out simply can't meet. Government grants are great, if you can find them and qualify for them, but that process can sometimes be quite challenging as well.

In addition to having little or no money as a new entrepreneur, you also have no equity and, for the most part, no experience of being in business for yourself. With such a lack of security, you are an investor's worst nightmare. I like to call these three crucial elements—money, equity and experience—the holy trinity of "no way," and I certainly received my fair share of "no ways" when I was developing my first successful business. But there was also no way I was going to give up the search for financial resources without a good struggle.

Regular lending institutions (primarily banks) have cookie-cutter requirements, meaning that if you don't fit their mould, you won't even be considered for a loan, regardless of how great your business idea might be. There are some entrepreneur-friendly banks that have more lending flexibility, but they still have requirements.

For various reasons, all the banks in my area turned me down flat. I had a solid business plan, with hundreds of pages showing my vision and how I intended to make it a reality step by step, but still none of them would give me a loan. Most of their concerns, I felt, were really excuses for them to say no. They would say: "The industry giants won't let you take a piece of their market; they will crush you"; "You don't have the security to back up our guarantee"; "Your product is not high-tech enough"; or "Your vision is too ambitious and will take too long to realize." Anything but yes.

I remember one time in particular when I submitted an application for a loan of $10,000. I had gone through a lot of due diligence with a panel of industry experts who were responsible for approving these loans. The $10,000 was part of a program to help local businesses that they thought had a chance of succeeding with a kick-start. I felt that mine was one of those businesses. After many meetings, the decision came down to a choice between my company and a landscaping company. The other company got the loan. Their reason for rejecting my application was that Hallmark or another large company in the field would never allow me to penetrate the industry.

The reasons given for refusing a loan varied, but ultimately, the reasons didn't really matter. The harsh reality was that I was not getting any money from traditional lenders. I would have to try something different. So I turned my focus to government grants and purchased a $500 book that guaranteed I would be able to find the funds I needed. I quickly learned that I didn't fit any of the eligible applicant categories. I was not a member of a visible minority, I was not a farmer, I was not in a not-for-profit organization, I was not aboriginal, I was not a high-tech company, and so there was no money available for me. The funds were targeted funds to meet obviously predetermined markets or individuals, something that I, as an eager new entrepreneur, hadn't dug deep enough to find out in the beginning. This was another disappointment, a waste of money and time, and another case of frustrating growing pain.

## When raising money, having an idea means nothing if you cannot demonstrate interest from the market, ability to deliver and how an investor will get a return on their investment

I was running out of options and getting desperate. Over the next few months, I began micromanaging my costs, and although it was very tough for me to do, I swallowed my pride and asked my friends and family for small sums to help cover these basic requirements. How much money did I need to get a purchase order fulfilled? How much did I need to buy a new computer? How much did I need to ship a package? The list went on and on. Instead of being able to focus on business development with proper funding in hand, I had to spend every single day chasing after money. This was draining, and it was holding me back. Every day I gave towards chasing money was another day lost from making a sale or building my business.

Even though I was desperate, I refused to settle for anything I was uncomfortable with. I'll never forget one meeting I had with four potential investors. Three of them grilled me, asking one question after another. The fourth, David, did not say much, but instead watched me with interest. The others asked about market size, competition and my desperate funding situation. They described impossible scenarios and demanded to know how I would react. They insisted that I answer on the spot. I did, without hesitation. Eventually, they were ready to make me an offer: $400,000 for 80 per cent of the company. This was four times what I was willing to give up, but I was about to learn that that wasn't the worst of it. **As part of the deal, they**

If it doesn't feel right, walk away

**wanted me to bankrupt my current company and shed the other investors.**

I was shocked. These other investors weren't providing a lot of money, but their contributions were valuable to me. Just the fact that they were willing to support me when I was at such a low point mattered so much more to me than the money. If not for them, I would never have been where I was at the time. Besides, these other investors were my family and friends. Despite my best efforts to convince these three potential investors how important these relationships were to me, they simply did not care.

In the end, **I had to say, "No deal."** They weren't pleased. Indeed, all of them, except David, became visibly upset. They told me I was crazy not to accept their deal and that nobody like me would ever again get an offer like this. Their reaction told me every-thing I needed to know. The fact that they got so upset proved to me that they were very interested in what I

Be able to say "no"

had to offer, and so I knew that others would be as well. It also told me that these people were loan sharks, not the kind of people I wanted to deal with, and that no matter how desperate I might be, I could never take their money. I couldn't sacrifice the trust that others had put in me, and I told them so.

After that meeting, I targeted everyone I could think of—everyone, that is, whom I considered to be fair and honest potential investors. Day after day, besides pursuing family and friends, I would make proposals and give presentations to prospective inves-tors. I explained my company, showed off my vision and talked about my successes. Bit by bit, I would sell off stock in my com-pany, from $1,000 to $5,000 at a time, and bit by bit I diluted my own interest. Although I had little success with these efforts in the early years, eventually I was able to raise over $3 million. It didn't come easy.

It took me years to raise the kind of money I needed to allow me to start focusing on business development, but I did it while still protecting everyone who had invested in me before. Along the way, what I sacrificed in money I gained in credibility and experience. My shareholders were impressed that I didn't sell out. And I learned to look at an investor's character before making any decisions. How they treated others, how they handled stress and what they were willing to sacrifice when things went wrong told me whether or not I wanted them on my team.

Ironically, that meeting with the four potential investors, although extremely unsettling and unsuccessful at the time, did later lead to some significant investment. About a week after the meeting, David called me to let me know that he respected my decision not to sell out my company and those who had trusted in me. The kind of person leading the company was an important consideration in his investment decisions, and I had shown I was the type of person he liked investing in. Part of an investment, of course, is in the product or service, but a major part is the company leadership. If investors can trust you and have confidence that you will do whatever it takes to protect their money, they're in.

As a result of my stand at that difficult meeting, David later became an investor, mentor and friend—someone who has always been helpful and fair to me.

# The Squeaky Wheel

There are times when, in the interest of fairness, you have to fight a little harder and dig a little deeper to stand up for yourself. Sometimes the squeaky wheel really does get the grease, even if you wish it didn't have to be that way.

Although I didn't have much luck with government grants in the early years, more recently I did, but not without navigating through a few twists and turns along the way. I had heard about a grant program, the National Research Council–Industrial Research Assistance Program (NRC–IRAP), which was designed to provide companies in Ontario with funding assistance if they met certain conditions. I looked into the conditions and found that I not only met them, I was a great candidate for the program. I met with an IRAP consultant who discussed the program in detail with me. He told me the funding would only be available in April of the following year, as the disbursements for the current year had already been issued and there was nothing left. I would need to assemble a proposal for the project I wanted funding for and have it ready for them by early January/February at the latest.

Several months later, around mid-August, I met with a representative of another financial institution, the Business Development Bank of Canada (BDC), a bank established by the federal government to help businesses grow through mentoring and financial support. During that meeting, the BDC representative mentioned that one of their clients had just received funding through the IRAP program. I expressed my surprise, since I had been told they were not disbursing funds until April. "Not at all," he said. "They have already started and at this rate will be out of funds by April."

## Obtaining financial support is possible for a new business, but be prepared to go through many roadblocks along the way

Immediately after that meeting, I contacted the IRAP consultant, and he assured me that I need not submit a proposal until January/February. **I was dissatisfied with this response, so I decided to contact his boss.** To get a clear and honest response from him, I decided not to mention I had been working with one of his consultants. He confirmed what the BDC representative had said: that the IRAP program was indeed starting to issue funds and that I should

Someone else's agenda might not be the same as yours

already have had a proposal in to them in order to be considered. Had I not been misled, I would have had my proposal in months earlier when I first met with their consultant. Now it was too late.

I tried to contact the consultant again, sending him several emails and leaving voice mail messages, but received no response whatsoever. I had heard before that this kind of horror story was typical of granting agencies. The process for approvals was loose and really left it up to the individual consultant to decide which applicants would be allocated funds and which would be turned down. Unhappy with this situation, I decided to contact the president and vice-president of NCR–IRAP. I laid out all the facts about what had transpired, and expressed my strong dissatisfaction with a process in which Canadian taxpayer money was being allocated with no really fair way of reviewing and approving candidates' applications.

Within a day, I received an email from the vice-president, indicating that the matter would be addressed. The following day, I received a call from the same consultant who had ignored my many communications earlier. He wanted me to meet him. He had good news: I was being awarded a $90,000 grant! I used the money to help cover several employees' salaries over the following year. There are times when the squeaky wheel really does get the grease, but in this case, the result did not sit well with me. I felt that the only reason I got the funds was because I had complained. The process itself should have awarded me the funds, which I felt I was warranted by the criteria established by the program. It did not.

# Beware the Wolf in Sheep's Clothing

There are people who prey on inexperienced businesspeople with promises that seem like a solution to all their problems. Think through what they are offering you and ask yourself if it makes sense. If it looks too good to be true, it most likely is.

Although I was not successful in getting any big investments in the early days of my business, there was one occasion when things looked very promising. As a young entrepreneur with no money and no personal assets, I had searched out dozens of companies looking for investment, but for all the searching I just couldn't find a partner willing to come on board with me. Until one day I got the call that I had been dreaming of: the president of a capital investment firm in Ottawa was phoning to let me know he could probably help me with financing and wanted to meet with me.

We met the next day in front of a university bar, and I knew as soon as I saw him that he was the prospective investor I was meeting. He looked like success. He was leaning against the side of his flashy sports car, dressed the way I thought a businessman should dress and casually tossing his keys. He told me he had helped many young businesspeople like me to get their businesses off the ground and make lots of money—millions of dollars! He proposed a deal: he would work with me to help me raise $500,000 and he would only get paid if we succeeded in getting the funds. During the time that he worked, he would bill at the rate of $1,500 per day for his time, but I wouldn't have to pay him anything just yet. He would work for free until the entire half-million was raised. During this time, a university student he had hired would work with me to develop a prospectus and complete all the required financial documents.

To an eager young entrepreneur who, so far, had struck out on every one of his funding searches, this seemed like a reasonable arrangement. He would work to raise the money I needed and it wouldn't cost me anything until it was all raised. I couldn't lose! So we moved forward and put together a contract containing all these key points. We were in business together.

It so happened that, around the same time, I had started the negotiations referred to in the previous section with a branch of the Business Development Corporation (BDC) for $100,000 to help me get my business off the ground. This deal was under review and had not closed yet, and I had no idea if my application would be approved. Had I known a month later that it would be approved, I would not have signed with my new "partner." Shortly after I got word that the financing had indeed been approved, he called me. He asked to be paid the per diem amount we had agreed on, which by then totalled $45,000. I told him I didn't see how he could claim to be entitled to a penny, since I was the one who had done all the work to get this financing and he had not participated in any part of the process with BDC. Not to mention the fact that he was nowhere near the $500,000 target we had settled on. **After a heated discussion, he slammed down the phone, for the first time showing me his true character.**

If it's too good to be true, it probably is

The next day, I received a hand-delivered letter from his lawyer. I was being billed for the full amount, and if payment wasn't made immediately, legal action would be taken. It was time to hire my own lawyer. He reviewed the paperwork and confirmed my suspicions: I was in the right, and my generous fundraiser was a wolf in sheep's clothing trying his hardest to take advantage of my lack of experience. We faxed over a document stating our position and, literally within minutes, received a response from what could only be his in-house lawyer. "They've been through this before," my lawyer said, noting the quick response. "They know exactly what they're doing." I decided that I needed to talk with this man in person, so I went to his office. To my surprise, his lawyer stopped me at the door, saying that I could speak with the president in court. This struck me as rather odd. I had thought that, in those kinds of situations, lawyers usually want to settle out of court at any chance they get.

## If something seems to be too good to be true, it most likely is. Tread carefully!

I had always believed that if I treated people with respect, I would be treated the same way, but this was anything but respect. This man was trying to intimidate me and take advantage of me. He was lying, attempting to steal from me. He knew as well as I did that he had done nothing to raise any funds for my company. He had had his student create some documents, but that was it. No meetings with investors, no opportunity to present my company. Nothing. I was upset that he was expecting to get paid from the results of my efforts while doing virtually nothing himself. We had a formal agreement, and the details indicated clearly how and when he was to get paid. My lawyer acknowledged the validity of my case, but, as he saw it, if this went to court, it would be all up to the judge, and it would be hard to tell which way the decision would go. **I would have to pay legal fees**, and because the other party had his own in-house counsel who actually appeared to be involved in the scam as well, they could run my legal bill up to the point at

Be careful of legal action. It can be expensive.

which I would end up paying much more than the amount he was asking for. Considering the relatively small amount of money he was requesting (although it wasn't small to me), it might be cheaper to simply pay him off than to go through with legal action.

I met with my two shareholders, and we decided we would meet with this man and his lawyer to talk about the issue. At this meeting, he was a completely different person from the one who had offered me such a generous deal: he was now cold, heartless and interested only in getting the money he wasn't entitled to. After several hours of heated discussion, my other partners and I talked over the matter in private and decided it would be better to pay him off. He and his lawyer seemed unstable, and we were concerned that if this went to court it would drain what little money we had. It would also take up too much of my time when I needed to focus on business. Against my better judgment, and grinding my teeth, I worked out a payment plan with him, and we signed an agreement that voided and replaced the first one. Over the course of the following year, we paid off his ill-gotten $45,000 charge.

It was a painful experience for me each time we sent him a payment, and anytime after when I heard his name, particularly when someone mentioned that he was working on another deal. Years later, out of curiosity, I visited his website. I shouldn't have been surprised to see my company's name listed as one of his success stories. To this day, a decade later, that listing and the presence of my company's logo on his website drives me crazy. I tried many times to get him to remove them, but he never did. **I could make his life difficult, now that I am in much better circumstances, but why bother? All I can hope for is that "what goes around, comes around."**

Focus on what is important

At the end of the day, this was a growing pain from which I learned a very difficult but valuable lesson: it is okay to be trusting and respectful, but you have to be on the lookout for those who would prey on you, especially when you're young and still learning the business ropes. If it looks too good to be true, it likely is. Don't do the deal unless you are sure it is on the level.

# Help for Free

When you do not have money to hire the right people to support you, look to the schools. Cooperative placement programs exist everywhere, and students need practical experience.

Without qualified resources to support a vision, many start-ups have a hard time moving forward. Without money, resources are still available if you know where to look and how to obtain them.

Over the years of scraping by, I had little choice but to do everything myself—bookkeeping, sales, business development, marketing, designing, production and even janitorial services. I knew I needed to bring more people onto my team of one, but when you have no money, your options are limited. My brother had mentioned to me that when he was in school they had cooperative placements that were part of the curriculum and for a student to graduate, they had to participant in the placement program. This was a perfect way to start building my team.

I soon learned that most universities and colleges have these types of placements in one form or another. Qualifying to be able to access some of the cooperative placement resources was a little challenging at the beginning, but I was soon able to work my way through their requirements.

What I needed initially were a couple of design people to help me create my product designs. I was fairly proficient at it, but it was time-consuming and I needed to focus on business development and sales in order to keep moving my company forward. I met with a professor from a local college who explained how the program worked and how we could qualify for their program. The students actually had to decide where they wanted to do their placement, and most would go into an area where they had the biggest opportunity for employment afterwards. All I had to do was to sell my idea to the students.

During our first time around with the college, three students showed interest in what I was building with Disney and decided to join my team for their placement period. The way it worked, for a six-week term I would leverage their skills to develop whatever I needed. It was a great opportunity for them, and the best part was it was free for me at a time when I needed assistance the most. What ended up happening over these six weeks was that I realized the power of a team. We developed so many new designs, new marketing materials and so much more that I really did not want to let them go. So I didn't. I scraped up the funds and kept two of them on.

This experience opened my eyes to the best interviewing process. By having potential employees work for you for six weeks, you really are able to access their strengths and weaknesses and determine if they are a good fit for your company. Since they are not, in fact, employees, you do not have any obligation tied to compensation if you do not keep them on.

Because I have hired young people from these programs almost every year, I am now always asked if my company is interested in doing a placement, and of course I am. I don't look just for designers, though. I have sought students in the broadcasting, multimedia, professional writing fields and, until my company iPal Interactive Learning was sold, students in an Executive Master of Business Administration (EMBA) program with a local university as well.

I had known that the EMBA programs also offered businesses the opportunity to take on interns, but I found out that the rules were stringent. In order to qualify, I had to write a proposal describing what I would like the EMBA student to do for me. It had to be something that was tied to business and that would constitute a challenge for the student. My vision was to take iPal global, but I needed someone to help me build my strategies for each of the countries I wanted to go into. The student who took up my proposal would work with me and my team for close to five months, for free, to build my strategies. I assembled my detailed proposal and went through the approval process with the university. Not only was I successful in being selected as one of the proposals that students could choose, but I also had the opportunity to interview Mark for the position. Mark was full of energy and passionate in his work. We hit if off right away—he reminded me of myself. I agreed that I wanted Mark and Mark agreed that iPal seemed to be a great fit for what he was looking for. As with other placement programs, Mark was looking for potential work afterwards. I told him that if he did a good job with the development of my plans, there might very well be an opportunity for him with iPal. Did he believe me? I'm not sure, but almost a year after Mark and I started down this path together, we had been to India and Barcelona together as part of Canada's trade mission. He has been to China and Brazil as well. We have taken the plan and executed it, turning my idea, a free placement program, and our combined passions to make a difference into a global market. **Mark is now my international business development manager.**

Cooperative placement to employment

Leveraging a system to get the kind of staff that enables businesspeople like myself to further opportunities has turned into many win-win situations over the years, and I expect they will continue to do so in the future.

# A Team of One

When starting your business, you need to include in your plan the main staff positions you will have in your company as it grows. You will not likely have enough money to hire a team at the start, so to fully understand what you will need to do to develop the business, you need to think of an imaginary team and act as if you were in the roles of the positions on it. Later, when the team is in place, the smart entrepreneur will be prepared to take on any job in the company to help morale and support the team approach.

As was discussed in Chapter 3, an important aspect of planning your business—how to put the puzzle together—is being able to visualize what it's supposed to look like once it has been assembled. Projecting the main personnel positions that your company will require down the road is one important aspect of this process.

Determining the positions and sketching out their roles and responsibilities will help you see what needs to get done.

It is also important that this information be captured in your main planning documents, your marketing plan, your strategies and your business plan, both for your own use and for potential investors to see. When investors look at your business plan, they are looking for many things, including, but not limited to:

- Do you know what you're talking about?
- Have you done your homework?
- Do you understand the market?
- Are you preparing for the future?

Including the right managerial and staff positions in your plans is essential to being able to answer these questions. The last is especially important. Preparing for the future isn't only about forecasting sales and cash flow. It also includes the expected nature and growth of your team, your governance structure and management support mechanisms.

## Planning your future team today will help demonstrate that you understand where you need support to meet your growth

There will be times, at the beginning of your business, when you will need to act as if you were holding down all these positions in your company. You will most likely not have enough money to hire several people at the start to actually work in these roles. But you need to be able to imagine what it will be like when your enterprise is fully staffed. When I started my business, I was working on a team of one—me. But that didn't mean I had to act like only one. I treated my business as though it had five board members, three business advisors and a whole executive team, not to mention all the employees I needed for it to be successful. I wanted to make sure that, whomever I wanted to bring on board, be they investors, bankers, partners or employees, they would understand that I saw my company as bigger than just myself, even though I was doing everything.

Having an imaginary team helps you see through all the elements that you will need to get in place when you are in a position to hire a real team. When you perform each role, you need to think the way you would if that were your only position. You don't wear your hat as the president when you are working on sales. Think like a salesperson when you are trying to get new customers, and you will find that you will accomplish more. When I looked at what I needed from a financial perspective and started working out details for that role, I was able to establish the baseline for what I had to do until I could bring on a person to fill the financial role. In the course of building my company, I put myself in several different roles—everything from CEO to designer, to programmer, salesperson, accountant, lawyer and marketer. Building a team means that you need to start with just yourself and then add others when you can. Being part of a team of one helped me to build what I needed to be part of a team of 10, 20, 30 and more to come.

Of course, changing job hats is not restricted to an acting role in the period before you are able to hire staff. Later, when you have a real team in place, you still should be prepared to lead by example, and this requires taking on a number of roles. **At different times, I am the president, CEO, chairman, employee, supplier, customer, licensee, financial manager and even janitor.** After all, even though I own the business, the toilets still need to be cleaned. Most people would ask their administrative staff to clean up an office mess, but what does that do for the staff's morale? In the short time it takes me to clean up the bathroom, I gain respect and credibility from my team, a key factor in successfully building the business. I am not above them, and I want them to know that.

Be willing to do anything

It is important to understand the differences between the various roles you have to play. In board meetings, for example, even though I am also a shareholder, I have to make decisions that do not necessarily benefit me personally (and I have had to remove board members for not being able to do precisely this). Set clear rules for yourself and follow them. As soon as you start breaking these rules, you run the risk of getting into trouble.

# Everyone Can Use Help

No matter how sharp an entrepreneur you are, you cannot think of everything. Having a team of people in your corner that you can bounce ideas off of will increase your ability to make the most effective decisions. It is wise to establish a board of directors for your company right from the beginning.

You're never too old to learn something new, and you're never too successful to take someone else's advice. As soon as I was able to do it, I formed a board of directors for my company. You typically build a board with people who can help advance your company by providing the operations manager or president with help in making key decisions on direction, strategy, financial management and governance.

When I first started my company, I had no sales, but I did have a board consisting of three people: Rick and Chris, who were my first shareholders, and myself. Rick and Chris started off as investors, then both became board members, and eventually, when the company began to bring in significant revenues and investment, Rick became my chief financial officer. It was bumpy during the development of the company, and Rick and I didn't see eye to eye on many things, but what I liked most about him was that he was not a yes-man and he respected my decisions even when he didn't agree with them. It is so important to have people around you who are honest with you and are able to give you the cold, hard facts, good or bad. Rick is the type of guy I would have on my team any day.

Even though there were only three of us at that time, I found that decision-making was so much easier when I had a group of people acting as a sounding board for my ideas and offering their own input. There are, of course, challenges when the people involved in your board are also shareholders and employees. When the company started to grow, we decided that we needed to put some distance between our roles as managers and as board members. At that point, we established a different board, adding new people we felt we could trust to help us grow: Bill, Jim and Tony. I referred to them as "the three wise men." They were a great resource, providing both ideas and constructive criticism, and they helped increase my credibility. I asked Bill to replace me as the chair of the board when we increased the governance team to five so that I could remain focused on my other activities. Rick also stayed on this new board, but in a different role from before.

## Building the right support team around you will help ensure a more successful outcome for your business

As my business advanced, I had to advance my decision-making process as well. I looked to people with decades of experience in international sales, finance, business development and manufacturing to build a board of directors that would have the knowledge and experience to lead us forward. A solid team can contribute more than just decision-making. Shareholders, banks and other financial partners are comforted to see that you have strong, experienced people supporting their investments. It's also important to draw on people across fields relevant to your growth objectives. **The directors on my new board came from various walks of life: international sales, multimillion-dollar companies and financial management.** But they all had one important thing in common: they were strategic thinkers.

Surround yourself with key experience

There was one major fear that I had to overcome in order to move forward with a board of directors: the fear of losing control. In the beginning, I was afraid that by opening up my company to others, decisions would be made and actions would be taken without my agreement. But with experience, I realized that the team is there to help you, not replace you. Their advice and support allowed me to become stronger and build a more successful company. This also provided me with more focus.

# Say Nay to Naysayers

Negative people are everywhere. They can appear among family members, good friends, acquaintances, advisors, bankers and even spouses. These are people who say things to try to keep you from following your dreams. It is important that you surround yourself with people who give constructive criticism rather than discouraging and doubting advice.

There are many different kinds of people in our world, and the best advice I can give regarding this is to accept that fact. Just as there are people who like different foods, adopt different dress styles, follow different religions and adhere to different laws, so also there are people who think differently. Nothing wrong with that! Differences are what makes our world such a great place.

But, although I respect and appreciate differences among us, there is one type of person I do not like associating with: the naysayers. They are the people who say, "You can't," "Impossible," "You are not smart enough," "You will never be able to do that," "Why try? You will only fail," "You don't have the education," and other such comments that try to deter you from following your dreams. These people are typically negative-thinking, pessimistic, glass-half-full, conservative individuals who either cannot or do not want to see a vision or understand the steps required to get there. Some believe, "If I can't do it, what makes you think you can?" These are also the people who will not take risks.

It is not so much the fact that there are people who think that way that bothers me. What I have had a hard time with in the past is the fact that they do not respect my ideas or vision. They feel the need to voice their opinion on what they consider my mistakes and how they think I should or should not move forward. And if I don't agree with them, they will even argue a position completely opposite to my vision, trying to discourage me from moving forward instead of providing support. There is always a way to give constructive criticism while still providing support, but the naysayers

Stay away from naysayers

don't do that. They would rather make you feel you cannot reach your goal, perhaps because they feel they couldn't do it themselves, and this is their only way to get across their frustrations. Whatever the reasons, **these types of people negatively influence one's ability to move forward, and you should try to avoid them.** In the past, I have told anyone who has behaved like this with me that I am not interested in their opinions if they have only negative ones. They should keep them to themselves. If they don't, I make a point of not being around them.

But people can be conservative and non-risk-takers without being negative and discouraging. I have friends, Eve and Aaron, who are precisely like that. Far from saying anything negative about what I am doing, they are actually very supportive and provide me with a tremendous amount of confidence, even though they do not fully understand what I am doing. They have become very close, non-judgmental friends with whom I can talk about my business and whom I can count on to listen and offer constructive input and support without question. They may not know much about business and what I do, but they are always open to discussion. They have said many times that they could never do what I do, but that it was always neat to hear my stories about my successes and failures, and what I do to get through the difficult times.

I have often wondered what turns some conservative, non-risk-takers into naysayers while others, such as Eve and Aaron, are positive supporters of risk-taking entrepreneurs like me. I figure that it must have something to do with the naysayers' own ambitions, their inability to move their own ideas forward and perhaps their fear of trying and failing. Combine that with envy and pride, and the only way they can seem to deal with the subject is through negative comments.

Plan the risks

When I started my first business, my friends used to tell me that their spouses would never let them do what I was doing and potentially risk their family's well-being. **What most of these friends did not realize was that I plan everything carefully and that I take only calculated risks.** What they thought was taking a big chance was actually a planned event.

Of course, there were risks, but at least I had thought through what could go wrong and was prepared for any eventuality. After my company became successful, it was interesting to hear those same friends being asked by their spouses, "Why aren't you more like Brad?"

When I started my second successful business, iPal, I again ran into many naysayers, some of whom I had worked with in the past, telling me there was no way my company would be successful. A previous business advisor told me he had known of many people who had tried to develop an e-learning company like mine, and all of them had failed. By this time, however, I was well prepared for these kinds of comments. Far from discouraging me, they inspired me to work even harder to prove that I could make it a success, and in the end I did.

• • • • •

Just as I would advise new entrepreneurs to stay away from negative people, I recommend that they take a positive, forward-looking attitude with respect to their business goals. True, this is a bit of a cliché, but it is sound advice. **Don't just act positive, *think* positive, and believe that good things will happen if you continue to work hard and do not give up.**

Think positive

Without a doubt, a strong positive attitude has been a big factor in my business success.

When I was younger I leveraged my challenging personal situation and harnessed the negative energy into something positive. I could have easily chosen a different path, and I certainly had many opportunities to focus on the negative, but I did not. I focused on seeing opportunities and turning what others might see as issues or risks into getting the positive results I wanted. Going through those hard times and being forced to figure out how to survive enhanced my ability to see solutions in every problem. Being alone for so many years and being introverted forced me to look within myself and enabled me to see the need to be more outgoing and forthcoming. It helped me see the value of positive thinking. Many of my associates today cannot understand how I am able to see opportunities where they believe there are none, or how I can be so positive during times of despair. Living life one way makes you see it in another way. I lived and felt pain, suffering, fear and desperation, so it takes a lot to make we worry. Tomorrow will always come, solutions can always be found.

Stay away from the naysayers unless you are certain you have the strength and determination to put their negativity aside. Think positive and pursue your dreams!

# Hard Work Breeds Natural Talent

> It is not the talent you have, but how hard you are willing to work that will bring you success. This applies to business as much as it does to sports. If you are passionate about a business idea and are willing to put in the hours and work hard at it, you will become good at it.

Do professional sports players have natural talent? Most people would think they do, but I disagree. Athletes may have some abilities or traits that help them succeed, but they don't come out of the womb shooting hoops or kicking balls. They acquire their impressive sports skills primarily through plain hard work. They've spent a lot of time practising a sport that they love, to the point that it has become part of who they are. Malcolm Gladwell, in his book *The Tipping Point*, shows how almost all the superstars—in hockey, for example—are hard workers. Their success didn't happen by accident. Gladwell cites 10,000 as the magic number of hours of effort required to become great at something. It was only after these people achieved success that their hard work turned into what looks like natural talent.

It is the same with success in business. This is why most business books tell you that your likelihood for success increases the longer you are in business. **As you develop your enterprise, you have to put in the time; the more time you spend on it, the**

Work hard

**better you will be.** I have been told many times that I am a natural leader, that I'm talented at a lot of different things, but the reality is there is no natural talent to it. I work hard and try and try again until I get good at something. Perhaps it is my will to avoid failure that makes me try so hard, or maybe my competitive nature, but in the end it has nothing to do with natural talent. Over the years I have met several people who have read about my accomplishments and have attributed my success to my intelligence. When they say these things, I always reply, "Actually, I am no more intelligent than you. I work really hard and put in the time."

Many people try get-rich-quick schemes to avoid having to actually work. When I was younger, I tried out several of these concepts, such as a pyramid scheme, as discussed previously. In the end, I realized that these businesses never make it, and I would have to keep working if I really wanted to succeed. This is why, if you are truly serious about being an entrepreneur, it is so important to never give up. In order to be an expert and someday be perceived as a naturally talented person, you need to roll up your sleeves and put in the hours.

I have also been told many times that I'm a lucky person. I do agree that there is luck involved in life, but for the most part we create our own luck. I attended an event a few years ago where Donald Trump was one of the speakers. In his speech, he said something that really drove the message home to me about luck. I am not comparing myself to Mr. Trump in any way, but he mentioned that people thought he was a lucky man. His response to them was, "You are right. It seems that the harder I work, the luckier I get."

# 6

# So You Want to Develop a Business

# Outgrowing Your Garage

Developing your own business requires making sacrifices. These might involve your money, time, personal life, credibility and much more. If being in business for yourself were easy, everyone would be doing it.

Like many teenage rock bands, my first multimillion-dollar business began its life in a garage, which I totally renovated for that purpose. I raised the floor off the ground, sealed the cracks and insulated the walls so I would not freeze in the winter as I worked on packaging my products. As sales increased, I hired a close friend who had lost his job during the high-tech bust, and paid him right off the paycheque from my day job. Each day, Henry would show up in the confined space that used to house my car and work on assembling the products I had sold the day before.

Family support

Then he'd prepare them for the shipping company I had arranged to come by my house to pick them up.

**With sales continuing to increase, my wife and I decided to sell our house and move into another one**—as large as our limited budget would allow—outside the city. After a while, our new house also became crammed with materials, products, packaging and shelving to the point that the pillars and walls of boxes blocked out the sun and forced my wife and kids to manoeuvre carefully to get from one room to the next. This continued for several months, the whole operation transforming our beautiful, newly purchased home into a warehouse.

Was my wife thrilled with this situation? Not really, but she was supportive of my determination to build a business. Did I want to do this? Of course not, but if you want to develop a business, you must start somewhere, and sometimes that means making big and unusual sacrifices. The level of sacrifice required depends on the resources you have at your disposal. In my case, I had to start building my idea from my garage, and then the house, because I didn't have the resources to do anything else. I leveraged what I did have in order to save money on overhead costs, infrastructure set-up, fixed monthly expenses, storage and so on. It may not have been a lot of money, but when you're starting a business, every few dollars make a difference. As for wanting to go this route or liking this experience, only our kids enjoyed it. The maze of boxes provided them with endless opportunities for hide-and-seek and other kinds of play.

## Sacrifices are part and parcel to being an entrepreneur. You must know the limits of what you can afford to sacrifice.

Our sacrifices weren't limited to the space we lived in. Other aspects of my home life and lifestyle were also involved. When I was working with PMC, I had been drawing a six-figure salary. With my wife a stay-at-home mother and me the only source of income, the decision to walk away from that, and into a situation where my salary would border on the poverty level, was extremely tough. **I would not, of course, have walked away from my only paying job without first ensuring that I had enough income from other sources to cover staffing and household basics.** My risks always are calculated closely, with the odds usually in my favour. Becoming a full-time

Mitigate income risks

business owner meant that I would have to make personal sacrifices. But, if I wanted to seriously pursue my entrepreneurial dream and ensure that I could protect my family in the future, I had to go through this "short-term pain for long-term gain," as my friend Chris used to say at our workouts. This is what I told myself during these hard years when we were getting by on next to nothing. I would ensure that I had enough money to cover my mortgage for the most part, food for the family and, of course, gas to get to and from work, but that was it. We did not go out to restaurants. Nor did we entertain, travel, shop or do any other things that would cost extra money. More often than not, we would count our change to cover things like gas. When the bank threatened to foreclose the mortgage on our home on three separate occasions and I had to negotiate to ensure that my family was protected—even when things got *this* bad, I kept a cool head and kept moving forward.

The hardest part of all this was not the sacrifices themselves—I had been used to not having much during my childhood. The toughest part for me was the impact they had on my family, my wife especially. Not being able to buy Nathalie nice clothes or take her away on holiday was hard for me to handle. Seeing our friends going on vacations and having the money to be able to do things we could not was rough on her. She would never admit it, because she was always supportive of what I was trying to do, but still, I could see it was difficult for her.

I knew before I made any move to start my own business that, if I were going to succeed, I would have to give up some of the things we were accustomed to having. **But to be honest, the level of sacrifice required was much worse than I had ever anticipated.**

Expect the worst

# Bent but Not Broken

You can keep bending a twig over and over again, but eventually it will break. Just as with twigs, everyone has a breaking point. To be a successful entrepreneur, you need to know where that point is and, for the sake of your sanity, not push beyond it.

Sometimes, even good news can bring its share of stresses and challenges when your business is still in its growing-pains phase. Three years after start-up, my paper products business was beginning to see some modest development, but by no means had it turned the corner. All my extra money was tied up in the business. I was working flat out, with no free time and little time even for sleep. On top of all that, I had a family to support. I had a few customers whose orders I was able to fill from my home "factory," but even this level of operation took an all-out effort.

Then, quite unexpectedly, I got a purchase order from a Toronto distributor: 80,000 pieces to be shipped before Christmas, which was three weeks away. I would need to buy all the raw materials, but I didn't have a warehouse to store them in. I didn't have the money to rent a warehouse. I didn't even have staff to assemble the product. Altogether, this presented a lot of problems to be solved in only three weeks. But I wanted it so badly. I wanted my product distributed across the country, and I wanted companies to start hearing about me. I wanted to build a career, to prove that I was serious, that I wouldn't quit. Failure to fill this order would have been devastating. Success, on the other hand, would mark a significant breakthrough. Needless to say, despite the huge challenge, I was thinking in terms of success.

I couldn't turn it down. My house would just have to become both factory and warehouse. Making decorative collapsible gift boxes was a multi-step process: it involved assembling the top and the bottom, sliding them into a thin bag, adding a printed cardboard header and stapling it all together. Nothing was automated! All in all, this single order would come to 240,000 staples and some very sore hands.

Raw materials started to show up at my house by the truckload. During the first week, several friends and family members came over to help. Day after day, we worked from six in the morning right through to five the next morning. After a while, friends and family stopped coming around, leaving just three of us—my wife, my brother Keith and myself—to continue the work. Meanwhile, the trucks kept coming. Skids of raw materials filled the front laneway. I felt like Sisyphus, condemned to roll a boulder up a hill for eternity. As soon as we had almost used up one mountain of materials, piles more would arrive for us to start on. **Every room of the house was packed, floor to ceiling, with raw materials totalling more than 2,000 cases. They were so heavy that eventually the floor became warped under their weight.**

Sacrifice is required

After one week, we had assembled 10,000 units, leaving 70,000 more to be done. No staff, no time, no sleep and no money. It was three in the morning, and I had passed out from exhaustion, sound asleep with a stapler in one hand and a polybag in the other. I woke up to find someone shaking my shoulder. My brother was leaning over me, laughing. "Brad," he said, when I was awake enough to listen to him, "if you're ever going to finish this order, you need more people."

I knew he was right, but I was too tired, too frustrated and—I admit now—too proud to respond, so I just resumed my stapling. It didn't last long. My brother pointed—while still laughing—to the pile of materials and products filling the dining room, even covering the windows so that we wouldn't "be able to see any light when the sun comes up." I had already hit my maximum stress level, so I couldn't do anything but laugh along with him. Even though I had put all my money and energy into this order, **even though I still had a mortgage and bills to pay, and food to put on the table, it felt good to laugh.**

Laugh even when you hit bottom

When I woke up later that day, I started making phone calls. Eventually, I found a company that specialized in renting out people. They could help with whatever I needed. Unfortunately, this presented one last challenge. By this point, I was completely out of money, and they wanted me to pay up front. All I had left was the last payment for my mortgage, and equity in the house, which I made sure we never touched. I sat down with my wife—always my most important business partner—and we decided to extend our mortgage so that we could finish the order and make our money back.

Staff from the temp agency, 23 of them, showed up the next day and got to work. It felt a bit strange having all those people and all those cases of raw material filling every square foot of my house. Still, I was happy to have them there. By the end of the week, I had shipped all 80,000 finished products. Not only did I get paid, but the order was so well received that I got another order from the same company for 800,000 units the following week. Needless to say, that was another big challenge.

The risk, hard work and struggle involved in making this significant breakthrough had been worth it, and it paid off. I learned several lessons from the experience. How we perform through the most difficult times not only defines us as people, it also determines whether we make our way down the path to success or failure. I learned that there are times when it is necessary, and smart, to swallow your pride and change your course. Looking back now, I see it all as a test of strength and perseverance—a tough but valuable experience for a developing entrepreneur.

# "Stress Madness"

There is considerable pressure that comes with being self-employed. When things go badly in business, the stress can take a toll, producing in many cases a reaction of intense anxiety and panic. How people respond to highly stressful situations will have a big influence on how their business will fare.

Experiencing a stressful event with someone tells you a lot about them. "Stress madness," as I like to call it, is the intense anxiety—and, in many cases, utter panic—that people experience when they're on the verge of losing everything they've worked for. Most entrepreneurs encounter this many times in their career, and **how they handle themselves determines how well they will fare in business**. When you hit rock bottom, how do you deal with the fear of losing everything? Does total panic set in and impede or change your decision-making process? For the most part, for people I have worked with over the years, the answer is yes. I have seen a couple of instances where individuals under pressure have held strong and thought their way through a crisis, but more often than not, people I have seen in those extreme circumstances have lost the ability, at least briefly, to think and act rationally. I have been involved in situations where individuals' fears had become a distraction to my work, and I have had to calm them down with reassurances that I would make things work out.

Manage stress

There are degrees of stress madness, and the level and nature of people's reaction to serious situations depends on their tolerance level. I have observed that, when their business goes really badly, people are likely to react in one of four ways. Some immediately decide to bankrupt the business, shed the debt and start up again using whatever assets they can salvage. These people are almost always in legal battles with old suppliers and past partners. You don't want to be one of those partners.

There are others who blame everyone but themselves, make excuses for what went wrong, and who never take responsibility. This type of person is very hard to work with, and I personally do not like working with them. Playing the blame game is their only way of handling failure, and you can never depend on them when things get tough—more likely than not, they will run from problems instead of facing them head on.

## Understanding your stress levels will help you better define your boundaries so that you have an ability for measurement

Then there are the ones—commonly featured in television crime dramas—who completely lose their minds when they see their business slipping away and begin doing things they wouldn't normally do at all. Their fear of failure will drive them to break the law, lie, cheat or steal. In real life, sometimes even the most honourable person can turn ugly because of the stress. We all heard the news stories during the financial crash of people who were previously known as honest, but at some point made a big mistake and then tried to fix the problem by resorting to some illegal activity. One thing led to the next, and then they were in so deep that they thought their only solution was to keep doing what they were doing, the eventual consequence being huge fines and even jail time.

Finally, there are the people who manage to stay level-headed, work through their issues, try new approaches and negotiate with suppliers and creditors to make the situation work for everyone. These are the ones with whom you want to partner. You need to surround yourself with people who, during the hard times, will leverage their strengths and lessons learned from the failures to make things work.

I have worked with people who fit each of these descriptions, and the experience has taught me valuable lessons about managing my business. These have been especially useful in helping me define the qualities that make a good partner. One of the questions I try to have answered when I am assessing a prospective partner is how he or she will behave under stress. And when I talk to the references they give me, **I always ask about the person's stress tolerance as well**. If I can understand how a potential partner handles stress, I can figure out if they are going to be a good partner or not.

Find out about your team's stress management

A really good example of the kind of partner who handles stress very well is one of my previous shareholders, David, whom I introduced earlier. David owns many different types of businesses, real estate and other investments. Over the years, when I met with David to talk about how my company was progressing, he was always calm, even when I had bad news. David invested a lot in my company and, during times when sales were low and the company seemed to be on the verge of closure, David would work through my ideas and strategies with me, providing practical feedback and the support I needed—just the kind of investment partner you need when the going gets tough.

# Eight Days a Week

Being an entrepreneur requires dedication, hard work and long hours. Finding time to get everything done is probably one of the most challenging aspects of building a business. But with a little thought you can find the time—by taking advantage of any time in the day or evening when you can fit in a little work without sacrificing other activities. It's a matter of striking a balance.

The life of an entrepreneur starting and building a business is a very busy one. There never seem to be enough hours in the day, or days in the week. I found it difficult when I first started to develop my business because I didn't really know what it took until I was waist-deep in it. Once I put together the plans, the processes, the staff and the products, more challenges would present themselves, and the time that I thought I would have to focus on the longer term would be consumed with everyday management and administration. As your business begins to take shape, all the dozens of key drivers of success become ever so important, especially sales.

When you're an entrepreneur, the office is always with you. That can be a good thing, because it gives you the flexibility to work with your family close by. And if you love what you're doing, which I'm sure most entrepreneurs do, it's well worth it. But it can be a negative factor as well. You have the stress related to work with you all the time, not just during the day at the office. You can't really take a vacation or days off because you are constantly worrying about making sure you have enough money to cover the rent, your payroll and other expenses that are required to keep your business in operation. **I never wanted to work as much as I did, but in order to achieve my dreams, I knew the effort was necessary.**

Work long hours

To help keep me motivated, I used to leave a Post-It note on the side of my computer that said, "What is your competitor doing right now?" This was a constant reminder that, if I wanted to be more successful than my competitors, I would have to work twice as hard as they did, no matter the time or place. I needed to find a way to get things done, to put in the hours to organize my thoughts and strategies, market my ideas, develop new concepts and research potential opportunities. But with a full-time job, a family to spend time with, a home to take care of and social engagements, where could I find the time to work on my business? For close to two years I worked at PMC full time while building EasyWrapLines. Once I felt that my business had enough revenue to support my leaving PMC, I took the next step. I decided that instead of working 100 hours a week split between two companies, I would work the same hours in one and hopefully be able to double my revenue.

I started to think more critically about the ways I was spending my free time. Watching television is my favourite after-work distraction. As with most of us, it gives me a mini-vacation from my busy day and lets me think about other things (or nothing). I began calculating the number of hours I was losing every day by just watching television: on average, up to six hours, on and off, of doing absolutely nothing. Instead of giving up my TV time completely, I started working on my ideas at the same time. It was distracting at first, but once I got used to it, I became so much more productive: it was like I was working two full-time jobs. The best part was that it didn't affect my family time. The kids were right there beside me, and when they needed me I could easily switch over from work mode to Dad mode. **I started to see a better balance in my life, jumping from playing games with the kids, making dinner, spending time with my wife and being productive while I relaxed.**

Find a balance with work/family

After I mastered TV-time working, I started to notice more opportunities during the day to work. On vacation, for example, at the beach with family or the cottage with friends, I would get work done while everyone else was just reading or tanning. I would bring my notepad along and write down thoughts on how to improve my business, my products and my life. I have been accused of being a workaholic, but I don't think it's true. I still spend a lot of time

with my family, attending school events, having dinner together every night and going on outings and vacations. I'm so passionate about what I do that it doesn't seem like work to me. Second to spending time with my family, working on my business and my ideas is my favourite pastime.

When my wife and children read books, I work on my computer. Since I am not a big book reader, what else would I do while everyone around me reads? One year, my wife's parents told me I was not allowed to bring my laptop on our trip. My response was that, if they didn't bring any books to read, I would agree not to bring my laptop. At first, they didn't think this was a fair trade-off, since their books were for relaxation while my laptop was for work. Once they realized that what made them relaxed did not work for me, but working on my laptop under those circumstances did, they agreed it was not such a bad idea.

Over and over again, I hear people complaining that there simply aren't enough hours in the day to work on their ideas. The truth is that there are enough hours; you just have to look for them and take advantage of any time in the day or evening when you can do a little work without giving up on other activities. It's a matter of striking a balance. Once you can get over that hurdle, you will exponentially increase not only your productivity, but also your chance of success.

# Staying under the Radar

Don't give away your secrets until you are ready to compete. When you are building your business, know who your competitors are and try to stay out of their view until you are able to establish a good relationship with them or are ready to handle their competition.

I have found that in business, for the most part, transparency is a valuable asset. However, there are times when it pays to be guarded about what you are doing or planning to do. Many new entrepreneurs are quite secretive about what they're working on, and with good reason. Other companies, especially those already well established, are naturally keen to find out what a newcomer in their field is up to. Some companies can be quite determined in this pursuit and are not above taking advantage of an inexperienced business developer. As a new competitor, you don't want to give them any extra edge.

When I was developing my first company, I stayed under the radar as much as I could. I was so afraid that one of the giants in my industry would see what I was working on and produce a similar product. Since I couldn't patent my product, this was a real risk. For a long time, I was successful in protecting my products and plans, but I was still inexperienced in many aspects of the business, and not sufficiently alert to all the possible traps.

I was attending a trade show at the Toronto Congress Centre, showcasing my products and trying to drum up business. It was my first show, and I was excited and nervous at the same time. Since it cost me a great deal of money to be there, I needed sales. So, unlike many trade show people who just sit passively in their booth hoping someone will come along, I stood at the corner of my booth and engaged everyone who walked by. One of the people I stopped was the Canadian sales manager for a U.S.–based firm— let's call it Knock-off Inc. It was a company I had never heard of before that was quite large and specialized in paper goods and party products. The sales manager was very interested in my product line and asked all sorts of questions about where I made them, their design and what companies I was selling them to. She went on to say that they also provided distribution for companies like mine and she was interested in seeing if we could work together. When she started to talk about taking my operation from a local business to an international business, I became quite excited. Too excited, as I would find out later, and blinded by the possibilities.

Over the course of the next several months, we talked about strategies, packaging and my successes to date. I began to think that my years of hard work were about to pay off big time. But then, after several months of constant communication, she stopped returning my calls and replying to my emails. At that point, I knew that something was wrong and a panic started to set in.

I needed to find out what was going on, so I hopped a flight to New York City to attend a stationery trade show where I knew

Knock-off Inc. would be showcasing. This would be my first time at this show and, unfortunately, under all the wrong circumstances. The thought had occurred to me that they might have been setting me up in order to find out how I was operating and any plans I had for further growth. But I tried to stay positive. I told myself that maybe I had just missed their calls. Maybe their email system wasn't working properly. I just could not believe they would have used me to get what they wanted and then dropped me.

I arrived at the show sweaty and fatigued, yet still excited. I headed straight for their booth and there, in front of me in a full wall display, was just what I didn't want to see: decorative

Competition could be dangerous

gift boxes, in a dozen different kinds of packaging and designs identical to my own in every respect. **My worst-case scenario was now a reality.** I had put my faith in the other people's integrity, my products in the hands of a major competitor, and my future at risk of being destroyed. I searched frantically for the director of sales to demand an answer, but she was nowhere to be found. I made my way back to the airport, worried and dejected. I tried to think about what recourse I had, perhaps even taking them to court, but I was broke and I knew that this would only distract me from doing whatever I could to survive. It would take a very long time and cost a lot of money to pursue legal action, and there was no guarantee of success.

One of my biggest North American competitors had just knocked me off. I knew I couldn't compete with them. They had shelf space in every retailer. They had a more advanced distribution network and a client base that had taken decades to build. **My company was in serious trouble. And worst of all, it was all my fault. I should have been more careful. I shouldn't have trusted them so blindly. I should have known better.**

Don't make the same mistakes

I returned to my warehouse, where I had nine people working for me. I had a big decision to make. I knew that the sales I had been working on and anticipating through this company were gone. I also knew that a much larger business than mine was now a competitor selling everywhere we had wanted to have our products. It took me weeks to find the silver lining in this big, dark cloud, but I was not about to give up. Instead of dwelling any longer on what had happened, I decided that I needed to charge on and figure out a way to make sure it would never happen to me again. So I changed my direction and focused on strengthening my future.

# Marketing: A Numbers Game

Technology allows us to get our marketing message out quickly and to a wide market. To get the most out of the technology, it is best to focus and customize each communication as much as possible, specifically tailoring it for the intended recipient. After the initial message, provide something of value beyond the advertisement. And always follow up on anyone who shows interest in your service.

Technology has added a new element to marketing, giving us the ability to get our message out more quickly and to larger markets. How you tap into the technology will determine how successful you will be in getting your message heard. The trick is to use the technology smartly.

## Don't blind spam your target audience if you want to build a following

When the telephone was still a new invention, people were excited when the phone rang—every call was answered almost immediately. Today, however, is another story. After telemarketers realized the power of selling over the phone, people started to screen their calls. Email was just as exciting as the phone when it first came out. Today, however, marketers have to be more careful about how they contact you because they know that most emails, like telephone calls, are being screened out before they get to you.

Communication technologies can be very powerful when you know what they can offer and how to take advantage of their capabilities. With so many avenues in play—social networking, email, newsletters, websites, telephone, radio, television—it can be difficult to stand out. Finding an effective way to attract positive attention can play a big role in your success. My approach was to make sure that I was out there, not in your face, but in a manner to which people could relate.

When I started targeting my prospects, I thought through a marketing strategy and then focused on what I call "the numbers game." Using email, I would target as many people and organizations in my line of focus as possible with advertising material—but only once, and I would embed it in my signature block so that it would not get blocked as spam. Restricting this advertising contact to just the one time was important; otherwise it would look as if I was spamming them and I would likely be blocked from sending any more emails to these addresses. I would then wait a week or two and follow up with other materials, this time non-advertising material that offered them a benefit. The purpose of the first launch was to show the prospective customer what we had available, should they be interested and the time was right for them to buy. The follow-up contacts were intended to provide them with value. **Giving value without asking for anything in return helps add to your credibility.**

Help build credibility

The numbers game does not mean you keep contacting the same large group of people over and over until they get back to you, but rather that you try to connect with as many new people as you can from your target market. It is important to focus your communications and not just contact people randomly. If no one bites, then you move on to the next stage, providing them with some non-selling materials such as an article, a white paper, links to other resources or helpful suggestions. You need to make sure that each time your message goes out, it looks as if it were written or designed specifically for the person receiving it. Customize it as much as possible to include such things as the person's name, their company and even their position. To speed up this process I create a baseline email and save it in draft format. From there, I copy and paste it to create several hundred more exactly the same. When I am ready to send out an email, I open it up and tweak it. This may seem like a lot of work, but it is more effective than the alternative—mass-marketing tools to which you only add the names. This customized version does not come across as a mass-marketing email, and it increases your chances of success. It worked for me.

One of the most important elements in this marketing approach is the follow-up. When people get back to you with an expression of interest, follow up with them immediately. Trying to attract interest in what you have to offer is why you are doing the marketing. If you don't move quickly to respond to that interest, it may not be there when you return later.

A good illustration of this came in an experience I had a while back with a recent MBA graduate who was working for me for a short period. He had been struggling with marketing and sales in the past, so, to give him some practical experience in building relationships and learning how to drum up business, I moved him into a sales position and supported him by showing him how I did it. I walked him through the process I use and he went to work applying it. Within a couple of days, he received a response from someone who wanted to discuss our service. During a conversation we were having later in the week, he mentioned this expression of interest. When I asked what the person had said when he followed up, he said he hadn't done that yet; he was going to wait until the end of the week, because Friday was the day he had set aside for follow-ups. I realized I had forgotten to mention to him that, when your marketing efforts get people interested, you need to reel them in. You don't wait several days. What if they change their mind? What if they go on vacation on Friday?

What struck me as odd was that this should have been common sense. At this point, I realized that he was probably not right for a sales role.

In marketing, there is nothing more important than following up when someone shows interest. This is Sales 101 and part of the basics of being in business for yourself. **The numbers game in marketing is about connecting, not soliciting.** That is key.

Build relationships

# Social Media Butterfly

Taking advantage of social media networks can work well for businesses if they are willing to invest in the resources needed and focus on updating and maintenance and not just set-up. Simply setting up an account will not drive people to you. It requires continual entry of information that is of interest to your audience.

The more exposure you can get, the greater your chances of getting noticed, and when you're building a business, the cheaper you can get that exposure, the better. Today, nearly every businessperson is expected to have an online presence, and social media sites like Twitter, Facebook, LinkedIn, Biznik and many others make it easier and cheaper than ever to get your name out there and capitalize on market exposure. With my first company, I was unable to take advantage of these opportunities because they did not yet exist. Today, however, I'm lucky enough to have someone on staff to do my social networking, creating continual awareness about me, my company and our accomplishments.

It is one thing to have a presence in the social media space, but for this to be effective you must ensure that you have the people on staff to update and maintain the programs. Becoming and staying a successful social media butterfly requires a lot of time and effort. To do this effectively you need to have the right person, someone dedicated to this work and familiar with its operations and possibilities. When I considered hiring someone to be my company's social media person, I looked for someone younger than myself and more attuned to the social media world.

She began by assembling a presentation deck that detailed all the social media spaces and the relevant statistics around them. Next, she outlined the requirements for the development of a social media program that would include our company's key focuses. The details of this were important because the message you put out on Facebook is not the same as the one you would have on Twitter or LinkedIn, for example. Since the users of these spaces are not the same, each must be dealt with differently. **Before rolling out in each space, Kate put together a plan of how our online presence would look**, what we would post on the sites and how much time would be required to maintain the conversations.

Planning is important

Going into her second year now, she has developed and maintained a full slate of social media programs. She has created iPal's blogging site, maintained our newsletter program, set up multiple social media portals, each with its own target audience, all the while coordinating with my design team on the elements she requires.

## Communicating through social media still requires planning out your strategies

When I hired her, she was not an expert in the field, but then no one was, considering the relative newness of these technologies. I was willing to give her a chance, and through her efforts—including enrolling herself in several social media programs at a local college—she truly has become an expert in this field. Our online presence has become an important and successful element in our overall marketing effort, to the point where other companies are turning to us and asking about our social media program.

Technologies change so much, and it is hard to keep up with them all. I have learned as I have developed my businesses that there will always be change and growth. In order to stay ahead, you need to hire the right people who have the experience in the growth areas. I am astonished still today with how fast things are changing, but thankful that I have a team that is excited by change and interested in tapping into it.

# 7

# Learning and Maturing

GROWING PAINS ARE INEVITABLE IN DEVELOPING a business from the ground up. How you handle them, especially those that seriously threaten your operation, can play a big role in your survival and success as an entrepreneur. In addition to mustering the determination to pick up and continue, you have to learn from the tough experiences. And learning is not restricted to the early phases of development. Nor is it limited to crisis situations. Learning in business is a long-term affair and a significant factor in your maturing as a businessperson, as your business matures.

# Arriving at Disney

Surviving a near business disaster and not only living to see another day, but achieving new heights of success, requires that you recognize your mistakes and, if necessary, start over. Above all, it requires a willingness to try a different approach and to be open to learning new things.

**Do not be too trusting**

I never heard from Knock-off Inc. again, but the nearly disastrous experience they handed me did teach me several lessons. **I learned that I had been too trusting. I learned that, even though staying under the radar is a good strategy for a new business**, the focus shouldn't be on a single line of defence, but should cover all points. You have to really do your homework to learn all you can about the competition and the marketplace before talking with competitors in detail about your operation. That means securing the marketplace through good relationships, contracts and as many other techniques for limiting the threat of competition, and through barriers to entry. For those of you who do not know, barriers to entry are things that you have, such as a patent, a contract, an established distribution network or even control over product placement in major retailers—anything that prevents competitors from doing what you are doing or entering your market space. Securing a barrier to entry does not mean that you will not have competitors; it only helps to reduce their number and makes it more difficult for them to penetrate your market. Depending on the market you are in, this could involve locking up retail space, patenting a product, copyrighting artwork, securing exclusive distribution, and many more options. Overall, this very challenging experience strengthened my determination and taught me that I had more to learn more before I was truly ready for the big leagues.

To move forward in a way that would limit the threat of competitors damaging me in that way again, **I started to develop product lines that I knew other companies would not be able to copy**. Among other things, this meant I would have to obtain the rights to use copyrighted, very popular and well-known artwork from companies such as the Walt Disney Company, Marvel, Nickelodeon, Twentieth Century Fox, Warner Brothers, etc. In my original business plan, I had identified the need to eventually get rights when I was sufficiently established to meet these companies' requirements.

Learn
to adapt

I first approached Disney regarding rights in my second year of operation, but was turned away without getting even a meeting, because I didn't meet their requirements of a minimum of three years in business, a healthy cash flow of at least $500,000, proven market success, a distribution network and various other stipulations that I was told were required. I felt strongly that getting rights was the key to my survival, and Disney was my focus. In order to get their rights, I knew I would have to convince them that I had something worthwhile to offer and that I knew what working with entertainment companies was all about. I needed to be able to prove that I was used to working with licensors, that I already had market results and that I had credibility.

To meet those basic requirements—and, hopefully, obtain licensing rights with the largest entertainment company in the industry—I decided to first go after the smaller ones. When I presented our story to some of the smaller entertainment companies, they loved our products and were willing to work with us. It soon became obvious, however, that working with licensors was not easy. Because they had so many contracts awarded to their distribution partners, product lines were also limited based on the

**Look for the opportunities**

category you fell within. **I realized that, if I were to focus on a single product line within a category instead of the category itself, the entertainment companies would be much more willing to negotiate.** From there, I started to understand how licensors set up their contracts with partners like me, and I realized that I could leverage those contracts to get more, with other entertainment companies.

Altogether, this credibility-building and learning period was a very successful time for me even though I was not making any money and the bills were piling up both at home and at work. I knew that if my plan worked, I would be in a much stronger position than I had been before I was knocked off stride. After nine months of no sales, and on the verge of collapse, I was finally able to secure a meeting with Disney.

I did not come away from that initial meeting with any rights to Disney products, but in that discussion, and the many meetings that followed, I was learning more about the licensing business all the time. In particular, I learned what contractual obligations the entertainment companies had with their current partners and, with that information, was able to see where I might have a chance of securing some rights for my company. Areas that were really not well marketed or supported by the entertainment companies' partners were the ones I would focus on in my presentations. I figured that if I were able to get one product that no one else seemed to want, I would be able to leverage the credibility gained with that to get more products and more opportunities. The licensors would then see my company as an opportunity to make money and would show interest. From meeting to meeting, I would then use their interest to generate interest from the other companies, leveraging one against the next, until I reached the tipping point and became a recognized and respected player in the industry.

The painful, eye-opening experience with the company who had stolen my product concept had forced me to change and set out in a new direction. Change is never easy; it moves us from our comfort zones into the unknown, and so we are sometimes slow to embrace it. But it is important to make changes, even when they are not forced on you by a nasty turn of events. Companies that do not change with the times will be left behind, so it is important to adapt, to always consider what is going on around us and what we need to do to make sure we're moving in step with new technologies, changes in the law, the emergence of new competitors and any other elements that can promote or hinder success.

Knock-off Inc's activities had forced me to make a major change in direction. More importantly, they opened up a valuable learning chapter for me, one that would lead to a productive relationship with the largest company in the entertainment industry, Disney.

# Working with Competitors

One of the more useful skills the new businessperson has to learn is how to work successfully with competitors. This is a delicate balancing act precisely because they are, at the same time, both competitors and companies you want and need to work out deals with in order to advance your business.

On the one hand, working successfully with competitors can mean strong growth for your company. On the other hand, failing to handle the relationship carefully could mean a real setback. This is especially the case with the very large competitors, who, if they choose to act, can stop your operation dead in its tracks.

Early in my business development, before I secured the rights with Disney, I had approached other companies, trying to work out arrangements to grow my business. I was achieving success with these efforts, to the point where I was creating market disturbance through our new product lines and becoming a bit of a concern for some of the larger companies. One of these was Hallmark Canada, another big player in the paper products industry, with whom I had had an earlier experience that did not end in my favour.

At that time, I had approached them about partnering with my company to distribute my Nickelodeon gift box line. The director I met with was quite enthusiastic about working with us and said she would speak to their VPs about us and our next steps together. Since they did not have the rights for Nickelodeon wrapping products, but their main competitor, American Greetings, did, I assumed Hallmark Canada would have been thrilled to work with us. When I didn't hear from them, I emailed, called and left messages for the director I had met. For several weeks I called but got no response. I became concerned, and later found out I had reason to be. Shortly after my meeting with their director, Hallmark Canada had been calling around to all the licensors trying to add gift boxes to their wrapping contracts. Instead of seeing us as an opportunity, their VPs saw us as a risk and wanted to make sure I would not get any more rights from licensors they had relationships with. From this experience, I learned to develop more stringent agreements with the people with whom I entered into discussion, such as non-disclosure and non-competition agreements designed to ensure my interests were protected. I also learned, again, to be more careful and less trusting with large competitors.

## In business trust is very important; however not everyone has a moral compass, so trust with a signed NDA is even better!

Two years later, as my company was making noticeable inroads in the industry, I met the president of Hallmark Canada. Before, they thought we would not be able to get any serious market traction, so they ignored my interest in a possible working relationship. They had underestimated my persistence in getting our product out there and working deals with anyone who would meet with me. Now, they saw me as a thorn in their paw and needed to figure out a different approach. So the president was coming to my office to discuss how we might be able to work together. I was apprehensive. I wanted to make sure that unpleasant incidents from my past were not repeated.

As I waited for the Hallmark Canada president at the airport, my team was busy at the office, preparing for his visit. In a strategy that I would employ later on a bigger scale with Disney, they were making a few adjustments to give the impression we were a larger operation than we actually were—flipping over every piece of paper on our walls so that our biggest competitor couldn't see what we were working on, and **putting up more blank pieces to make it look like we were more active than we really were**.

Leverage perception

I met the president at the airport. I had done some research on him and, to break the ice, I joked that he was the perfect man: a six-foot-tall, dark, handsome fellow who had gone to Harvard University on a football scholarship. It seemed to work, and he started to laugh. We both respected the fact that we were competitors there on business, each with his own objectives. Under different circumstances, we might have been friends. (In fact, he and I still keep in touch today. After that experience, I came up with a saying that I try to keep in mind when I feel threatened: "You are only my competitor if we can't figure out how to work together.")

At the office, I showed him around and, before long, he asked about the mysterious pieces of paper all over our walls. I explained that we were in the process of developing several new programs, and that these papers represented the different graphics and programs we were about to launch. I could sense that his perception of our company was changing.

As his view of us changed, I became more confident about the outcome of our meeting, hoping that he would decide to work with us instead of against us. Hallmark is a multibillion-dollar company, so competing with someone like that is dangerous. **No matter how many great designs we produced, they had the financial means to crush us.** They could have wiped us out if they wanted to, but it turned out they didn't. We, unfortunately, did not do a deal then, because it was not right for my company. His offer was basically designed to protect Hallmark Canada's interests and restrict ours.

Stay out of crushing range

After our meeting, I was invited for further discussions at their office. When I went there a couple of weeks later, I noticed a large grid on the wall outside the director's office listing all their main competitors and what licence rights each of them had. They were keeping track of their competitors' moves so they would know which ones to go after. I returned to that office a couple of years later, after securing the rights with Disney and many others and after importing roughly 15 million units into the market. This time, Hallmark had invited me to discuss how we could work together again. When I walked onto their main floor, I saw the same list of competitors up on their walls, but with one difference: there was now an entire wall dedicated to my company. It reminded me how much I had learned about the business and accomplished in only a few years.

Despite my earlier apprehensions, I really enjoyed my dealings with the president of Hallmark. We never did work together, but we did carry on a kind of love-hate relationship from time to time. I would see him at trade shows, walking with his team of creative people from booth to booth. They would spend a significant amount of time in my booth area while the president and I talked. We were proud that such a large company spent so much time trying to understand us and compete with us.

I have worked with many competitors in the past, and the only instances that worked out well were those in which the companies were honest with me and were willing to give something back in order to get something. With those companies, both of us came away from discussions as winners. Unique Industries, a U.S.–based company with offices in several countries, including Canada, was one of those.

I approached them to see if there was an opportunity for us to work together on the sale of my products through their channel in the U.S.. My overall goal was to establish a better market penetration in the States as quickly as possible, and the only way to do that was to partner with someone like Unique.

The overall market in the U.S. and Canada is divided into many channels, the main ones being the mass market, the discount market, the grocery/pharmacy market and the independent market. Working directly with the buyers in the first three of these was feasible because they would purchase for their entire chain and have the product shipped to between one and nine distribution centres. For someone like me, managing the logistics in this situation was much more viable than it would be with the independent market. This is one of the hardest segments to dominate because it includes thousands of ma-and-pa stores that require you to ship to each store directly. That is not an easy task unless you have both a facility to ship from and sales reps to take care of the relationship with the customers.

Unique Industries is one of the largest party store distributors in North America. It is family owned and operated, and its focus is the independent market. **If I could leverage my rights to gain access to their distribution network, I would be able to increase my distribution throughout the U.S.** and they would be able to increase their revenues and gain more retail space. So I contacted their president, Craig Novak, to see if we could work something out. I mentioned that I had rights for Disney in the U.S., and I knew from their catalogue that they did not. Craig was intrigued by my persistence and the fact that I had these rights. I sensed that he saw an opportunity right away.

Leverage rights for distribution

Despite this, when I flew down to Philadelphia for our first meeting, I was nervous about whether Unique would buy into what I was selling. I figured they would, but I had been taken advantage of by several other competitors in the past, so I was naturally a little apprehensive. But there was a significant difference now: I had secured rights with the entertainment companies, in particular the giant Disney.

## A competitor is only a competitor if you can't figure out how to work together

When we started to talk, one of the first things that came out of his mouth was, "How did you get these rights?" He was genuinely surprised. I smiled and said, "It is all about how you present it." I again expressed my hope that he could be one of my distributors in the U.S., selling to the independent market. He replied that they usually did not do deals with other companies and that they had complete control over their own product lines. With the deal I was proposing, I would own the rights and he would be my partner. He didn't really like that idea, but he liked the fact that I had licensed rights. He also wasn't really sure how we would work together, since we were both selling into the same stores, though not the same products.

I had been told several times that having these rights was like being able to print money. Only a few companies had the ability to sell these products, and this gave the seller a clear advantage. Craig knew this. I knew by the way he asked about my acquisition of the rights that he had been trying to get them for some time but had not succeeded. Since he did not have the rights himself, the opportunity I was presenting to him would accomplish two important objectives for his company. First, they would be able to start selling licensed products, and second, they would gain additional credibility to leverage when they went back to the licensors and sought more rights themselves. In the end, we worked out a win-win deal for both our companies. At the same time that I acquired rights in Canada for the wrapping products, Unique Industries got rights for the party products, both lines originally dominated by Hallmark Canada. We both saw Hallmark as a competitor, and being able to make Hallmark uncomfortable was another achievement we both could enjoy.

## Leveraging could be beneficial to not only you, but also your partners, clients and even competition

Craig was one of the most personable competitors/partners I had ever had the pleasure of working with. When we first met and discussed the possibility of working together, he had real reservations about the idea. In the end, we not only partnered, but built up a great relationship that included visits to his house, socializing and a memorable "competitive" game of Ping-Pong in the basement of his mansion. Business was still business, and unless the deal was right for Craig, he would not do it, but at least we had the ability to talk about it. Learning to build relationships, even with a competitor, is important because it can lead to partnerships and other opportunities so long as both parties are open to a win-win arrangement. Years after the closure of my company, Craig and I still talk.

# Perception and Reality

There are times when what a prospective partner perceives about your business is more important than what your business might be in reality. When you are starting out and the stakes are extremely high, there will be occasions when you may have to dig down extra deep for creative ways to maximize your limited resources.

Successful people want to work with other successful people. It's just that simple. If you are struggling, if you have no sales and no contracts, a company will not want to take a chance on you. As you are trying to establish credibility and build your business, you often have to push harder and do whatever is legally possible to squeeze the maximum out of your limited resources. This can mean taking steps to make sure whatever successes you have had to date are well publicized. It sometimes means having to push yourself to appear confident in business meetings, even though in some ways you are anything but. It can involve creating the impression that you are farther along the road to becoming a large, fully established business than you really are. It is unfortunate that we must take this sort of action in order to have a chance at success, but sometimes there is no alternative. The organizations we want to work with are really only trying to reduce their risks by ensuring they are working with entrepreneurs who know what they are doing and businesses that are financially stable.

In order to generate credibility and increase others' confidence, some new and small businesses engage in a kind of scene setting. They may set up telephone systems with multiple extensions to give the impression they have several people working for them when, in fact, their total staff might be only themselves. They include photos of themselves with important people in their promotional material or have their websites boast about high-profile customers with whom they have never actually dealt. In my case (and I suspect in the case of many successful businesspeople), pushing the limits sometimes led me to create the impression that my operation was bigger than it really was. I have never lied, nor would I ever do so. When due diligence is performed, and it always is, the picture I have presented aligns with the facts.

When I first started doing business with Disney, for example, they didn't ask me for any particulars regarding my staff and office size, and I certainly wasn't going to volunteer any. So I was able to avoid that tricky, and potentially damaging, first impression about the size of my company. I had to gain credibility through the months of extra effort put into working with them on product design. **Focusing on the assets I had and avoiding what I did not have was a key to moving the relationship forward.** The hard work paid off and I got an important first contract with this very large international company.

Focus on strengths

To begin with, Disney gave us the rights to gift boxes only, but I knew that if they assumed we were larger than we were, they might entertain the idea of giving us opportunities with other products as well. One day, my Canadian Disney account manager called to say that she and some of her co-workers wanted to come to my office, meet me and my team, see the office and discuss some potential opportunities. I made the assumption that the reason she was coming to see us at our office was because she wanted to check out our space and determine our capacity; otherwise we could have had the conversation on the phone. I was in a panic. The possibility of further opportunities with them looked promising, but if they saw my modest 700-square-foot office space and my handful of employees, there was a good chance she would conclude that I was too small to take on more responsibilities and would end the discussion right there. My mind was flooded with questions, and I could only think of one word: size. In order to remove the risk, I had to give her the impression, without actually lying to her, that we were much larger than we were. I needed her to come to the conclusion that we could support their needs, even though I didn't really know why they were coming down.

It happened that my office was attached to several unoccupied offices and an empty warehouse. I contacted the landlord and asked if I could have temporary access to the area adjoining our office so that it would look as though we had a lot of space to grow in. The only challenge was that we would have to tear down a couple of walls to make it look as if the spaces were joined together. To persuade the landlord to agree to this, I used the power of leverage: if my plan worked and Disney gave me more product lines, I would need to rent his extra space in the future. By the end of the day, I had over 20,000 square feet of space to show to Disney. We tore down sections of the walls and then transformed the additional office space into a holding room for our products. To complete the picture, we put down skids in the warehouse to make it look like a receiving and shipping area. We didn't have products to put everywhere, but we did have the perception of strong potential.

## Envisioning possibilities could make them reality

But that amount of space is only impressive if you also have enough people to work in it. I didn't, so I invited some friends and family to come to the office and gave them specific acting instructions for the day of the Disney team's visit. With their help, we found extra pieces of furniture for makeshift workstations. As I waited at the airport for the Disney team's arrival, my crew was busy applying the finishing touches: stacking empty boxes in the warehouse, setting up a boardroom and preparing to take up their stations. I'll admit there was a moment when I worried that I might have overreacted, but then I concluded that, even if I had overdone it, I had nothing to lose. If, on the other hand, I had *not* gone too far and they were planning to offer me something big, I had everything to gain.

When the team from Disney arrived, one of the first things they said was, "Wow! You have a lot of space to grow."

At our meeting in our big new boardroom, the account manager said she wanted to meet with me face to face before talking about a "significant opportunity" for my company. They were looking for a partner who could provide access to the "value channel," otherwise known as the dollar store business. It was a growing industry at the time, and certainly a desirable one to be in. She wanted to see if we had the capacity to meet their growth objectives. My assumption had been correct. The large companies were either not interested in the value channels or were demanding more from Disney to become involved with them. Instead of giving up on this potentially valuable growth opportunity, Disney thought it might be worthwhile looking at a smaller company that was easy to work with, grateful for the opportunity and still motivated by the entrepreneurial spirit.

# If you work hard, your hard work will eventually pay off, sometimes unexpectedly

Even though I was the third choice, I seemed to be the perfect fit. The account manager asked if I was interested in a contract, and of course I said yes, but I was concerned that the cost might be too high. She smiled. "Brad, we know you don't have a lot of money. We're more interested in someone who's motivated to work with us right now. Because of that, we're willing to give you the rights for free for one year." I couldn't believe it. The new product lines would give my company huge leveraging power. It was what we had worked so hard to reach, and now it was there, right in front of us—and for the first year, free!

I later asked myself if we would have been offered the same opportunity had we not taken the time to make our office and warehouse space appear to be much bigger than it really was. Possibly, but regardless, we helped the decision-making process move along more seamlessly by adding these elements to the picture. Perception, unfortunately, is important for new businesses.

Stay true to your moral compass

How one sets the stage to add credibility to that perception can raise questions about what's ethical. **I myself do not like playing with my ethics and find it emotionally draining when I am faced with situations where I must step a little over a line.** But, in the end, I have always taken comfort in knowing that my actions did not create any issues for anyone else. I did not cause anyone pain, discomfort or create additional work for them. Rather, having to set everything up created more work for me.

# From Acorn to Oak

> If you are trying to get the big deals closed when you are first starting out, forget about it. It is smarter to start small and gradually build your credibility. If you first prove that you are a good partner to work with, you will prime yourself for larger opportunities down the road.

Even though you may have a good product, or perhaps even the best product in its category, as a new business with little or no credibility, you will find it hard, if not impossible, to achieve huge success right from the beginning. By starting small and leveraging the few strengths and successes you do have—including your limited credibility—you have a chance to prove yourself and thus be ready for bigger opportunities when they come along. If most entrepreneurs are like me, they don't want to start small. But you definitely need to accept that reality, realizing that you don't have to stay small for long, especially if you have a great idea. You need to work with what you have and not expect that others will give you the world to move your idea forward because you are that good. I could have left my small office the way it was and tried to convince Disney when they arrived that we were the right partners; perhaps it would have worked. But I understood that, in reality, I was a small player, and this realization made me work harder to achieve what I wanted.

After the Disney visit, they had the comfort of seeing that we had the ability and the commitment to work with them and build up a market that they had never been in before: the value channel. As a result, they awarded me the rights for two additional product lines, and almost immediately my business grew significantly and rapidly. In less than 30 days after I got that second Disney contract, my sales reached over three million gift bags, representing $1.5 million. **But the seeds of that growth were sown earlier, when I was going after smaller entertainment companies to get rights** that no

Achieve success through previous planning

one else wanted. I needed to prove that I was able to work within the licensing space that was available to me, and the only way to do that was to obtain licensing rights. I knew Disney would not simply give them to me, so I started smaller. The successes I achieved on a small scale increased my credibility and allowed me to leverage even more and bigger opportunities when the time was right.

**When you build a house, you start with one brick at a time. It is the same with your idea. Start small and eventually your bricks add up to something much larger.**

Dollarama was the key to this increased credibility and the growth that later followed from it. It was a fast-growing dollar retailer that had a limited number of licensed products. When we met with them, they were thrilled at the prospect of being able to increase their lines of licensed products. Up to this time, licensed products were a premium line that could be found only in mass-market retailers like Toys "R" Us, Walmart and several others that fell into this category. Dollar stores were looked down on as outlets where customers went to purchase products of inferior quality. Dollarama's quality, however, surpassed all expectations for products typically found in dollar stores.

Just as important as my opportunity for contracts with Dollarama, if not more important, was my opportunity to get to know its owners. Through this close relationship, I learned how they had built their business and how I might be able to get opportunities with companies such as Disney. What started as a small opportunity was being leveraged to grow into something much larger and something I had always hoped for. Of course, my credibility in the field was growing as well.

# Leveraging Perceived Value

When you are faced with a big, complicated challenge, sometimes the solution is to find new, creative ways to leverage something you already have. That could mean using the credibility you have earned from a previous contract to win new opportunities and, with them, more credibility for your business.

With new opportunities often come new problems. When Disney agreed to give us the rights to a couple of wrapping products, I was excited, to say the least, but I was also terrified. I knew that there would be a lot of work required in order to sell, design, manufacture, ship, distribute and, overall, manage the process, the team, the quality, the finances and the risks. But the biggest question was: How could I get three million items produced and paid for? I had no money, limited credibility and no idea where I could get these products made. There are very few plants in North America that could manufacture anywhere near this volume, and most of them already had agreements with industry giants or were owned by our competitors.

I thought about the overseas market, but having never worked with anyone in that market, I would be facing a huge challenge by going there. I did search for manufacturing plants overseas and found quite a few I could have dealt with, but I still had the problem of how I would be able to pay for their services. If I really tried, I could have located an overseas supplier myself and tried to negotiate terms of payment, but to me, it didn't seem worth it; the risk was too great. The plant could turn out to be of poor quality. Or it might insist that I pay for everything up front for the first order until we were able to build a working relationship. There are so many horror stories in the industry about working overseas, and it always seems that when production goes wrong, the purchaser is the one that ends up out a lot of money. I didn't want that to be me.

My problem was a little more complicated than I first thought, which meant that I had to come up with a creative solution. I tried to recall everyone and anything that might help me to overcome this challenge, and in the process I thought of a previous client, and current competitor, who might be interested in working out a deal. Since that company had been producing gift bags for decades, they already had the relationships, the credit and the ability to make this happen. I figured that if I proposed that they become one of my distribution partners, they would let me use their overseas plants and leverage their credibility. It would take some time to negotiate, but in the end the products that I now had would provide them with an advantage over their main competitors. It would provide me with the ability to produce and distribute my products without taking on the financial risks.

The overall solution for me was to make them think they needed me more than I needed them. I had to be the one in control if I wanted to make sure that I got what I needed, which in this case was someone to help me produce my product and also provide the credit I needed so as not to have to pay up front. I decided to call the president of a company that had previously purchased my gift boxes. I knew I had an opportunity that most companies in the industry could only have dreamt of getting, but I also knew that they would not believe me if I didn't have proof.

To back up my claim, I brought my Disney contract to our meeting and allowed him to look through it. As he read, he saw that I had indeed secured the licensed rights from Disney for gift wrap, gift bags and several other lines which, for the last several decades, had been dominated by the Hallmark corporation. As he continued to read, his eyes opened wider with surprise and excitement. We started talking about what I was looking for from him, and I could tell from his nervous reaction that he would be willing to do anything to work with us. I set out the terms of a deal that would provide me with what I needed but would also give him a very good opportunity, one he could not turn down. It had to be a win-win; otherwise the deal would not work.

From his point of view, the deal meant his company would stand out in the market from its competitors. It would also give him additional leverage: if his customers wanted Disney wrapping products, they would also have to purchase his non-licensed products. From my point of view, it meant his company would provide me with access to his plants and give me the ability to leverage his company's credit to produce my other orders. In both cases, he would purchase products from me and then distribute them to his customers, while also producing what I needed for my customers.

This was a tricky deal to negotiate, but a winning one for both parties—a clear instance of leveraging the credibility earned with a previous contract into promising new opportunities and, over time, additional credibility. It also demonstrated an example of competitors working together and both benefitting.

# Sign on the Dotted Line

It's great to have agreements in principle, but they need to be put into signed contracts to ensure that both parties are protected and on the same page. It is wise to have contracts with a diverse number of companies, and as many long-term agreements as possible.

As all your hard work and long hours begin to bring you "good luck," you will come to a point where you are making deals with other companies. It is important that these arrangements be put into contracts, preferably long-term ones. Everything may seem fine when someone shakes your hand and says you can trust them, but the reality of all business dealings is that people forget the terms of what was agreed to, and some may not be as trustworthy as you thought. Having them **sign an agreement raises the dynamics of the relationship** to a point where they take you more seriously. Signed, written contracts also provide additional protection for both parties and ensure that they are on the same page.

Sign agreements

When you have contracts, you also have more opportunities for leverage. I found that once you get someone to sign on the dotted line, it becomes easier to generate interest and get even more contracts. One word of advice with contracts: keep it simple. For people who are unfamiliar with legal jargon, contracts can be confusing and even scary, not to mention expensive. Lawyers are salespeople too, and sometimes they will convince you that you need more than you actually need, in order to keep their billable rate as high as possible. I have had many lawyers charge me for the oddest things because they said they were needed.

During the final stages of the iPal acquisition, my lawyer asked me if I wanted to add a bankruptcy clause to the acquisition terms. This would be a clause ensuring that, in the event iPal declared bankruptcy, the company would still be required to purchase the company. My surprised reaction of "You're kidding, right?" sent the message that enough was enough. There was no way iPal was going to go bankrupt, so it was time to stop trying to squeeze every dollar possible out of the legal formalities. After spending hundreds of thousands on legal fees with my first company, **it became very clear to me that many of the extra items lawyers suggest are not necessary at all**. If you keep the language simple, you're ensuring that everything both parties need to know is clearly laid out and easily understandable.

Beware of professional service fees

# A legal process could kill a deal. Business needs to lead the process to ensure an agreement is win-win.

When dealing with new partners, you should make sure that they sign a non-disclosure agreement (NDA) and a non-compete agreement before you disclose your information or idea to them. Also make sure that they have the authority to sign on behalf of their company. If they refuse to sign documents that are designed to protect both of you, think twice about working with them. And note that the agreements should be designed to protect the interests of *both* parties. If they are slanted to the benefit of one party over the other, the deal is being positioned to fail right from the beginning.

After I have obtained an NDA, I move on to a letter of intent (LOI). This is usually a non-binding agreement, but it does help to move along the thinking towards a formal agreement. I have experienced the confusing situation that arises when the parties jump right into a formal agreement in which the terms and conditions just seem to be too complicated and the process too fast. **By taking slow, small steps, one at a time, you will be able to move through the deal** much more smoothly, with everyone feeling more comfortable along the way. The trick is to stay the course and make the people doing the deal feel that the process is straightforward and win-win.

Take one step
at a time

# 8

# Building Credibility

BUILDING CREDIBILITY IS ONE OF THE ESSENTIAL requirements for developing and sustaining a successful business. Having credibility means having believability and trustworthiness. People trust you as a leader, producer, marketer or partner—an all-round success in your business initiatives. Developing this trust does not necessarily have to cost money. It requires honesty, smarts and persistence. You can't force someone to trust you. Trust has to be earned, and it's not something that happens right away. It comes with proving yourself and following through on your word. Credibility comes with building that trust and reliability over time.

# Earning Credibility

> Possible ways to build credibility are many and varied. They range from emphasizing or enhancing one's personal approach, such as maintaining strong ethical standards, to developing or honing basic business skills.

The following is a sampling of some of the many lessons I have learned from my business experience that can help in establishing both personal and business credibility.

## Take a modest approach

I have worked with people who feel they need to run through their resumé every time they encounter someone new they would like to impress or whose respect they are trying to gain. They seem to think that rattling off a long list of their accomplishments and boasting about their successes will instantly bring them credibility. In my experience, this mode of operating is more than likely to be counterproductive. I have found a more modest approach to be effective.

For example, in a meeting with a prospective client for the first time, instead of giving a pretentious list of reasons why you're certain your product (or service) is superior to all others, it is better to give a quick demonstration of your product and talk about what makes it different. This can then lead naturally to a further discussion, if they're interested, in talking about other products and, perhaps, various work situations you have encountered and adapted to. Both approaches are self-promoting, but the second is much gentler. It focuses more on the credibility of the product (or service) than on the person promoting it, and it's more likely to engage the other party. It allows prospective buyers to find out about your accomplishments for themselves and come to their own conclusions about the value of what you have to offer. By all means, let the other party know of any big successes you have had, but do so in a manner that doesn't have you boasting about how great you are. And you should never talk badly about your competitors or others in general. Instead, always focus on the positives of your products or services.

## Tell the truth

As an entrepreneur, you expect to be trusted by people. In turn, you need to be honest with them. Of course, there may be times when you can get away with an innocuous "white lie." My rule of thumb when it comes to "white lies" is very straightforward: Does it make me question my ethics? I will not play with my ethics, and when I am put into a situation where I am forced to lie about something, I will not lie. When I do tell a "white lie," it is usually because telling the truth will cause someone else unhappiness or pain (without a benefit to them or me). Occasionally, I am the one who experienced the pain—a good example of this is when I first tried getting work in the field of business. No one would hire me unless I had experience listed on my resumé. But, essentially, the best policy is to tell the truth. It is at the heart of earning trust and credibility. And, of course, there is an obvious danger in lying: if you are called out on a big lie, or a bunch of small lies that have been built up, you will lose people's trust and you will lose business opportunities. Your credibility will be seriously weakened, if not destroyed.

## Be transparent

Closely related to being honest in business is being transparent. Sometimes, people express concern that I'm being too open, sharing too much about my ideas, successes, failures and future opportunities. But far from considering this a problem, by and large I see it as a positive attribute. Openness contributes to people's trust in you, letting them know there's nothing sinister going on behind the curtain.

Of course, there are limits to this openness. Prudence dictates that there are often things that your team, partners, customers or bankers don't need to know. Common sense must be used.

## Use the media

You've gone into business because you are confident about your product or service. Why not get the word out by writing an article about it? Look for associations in your field and try to publish in their newsletters or journals. This way, your peers will be aware of you and what you have to offer. You can also make use of press releases, newspapers, blogs, social media, conferences and local television spots. Of course, with this kind of self-promotion, you must remember not to cross the line from confidence into arrogance or pretentiousness.

## Be a leader

It's easy to copy someone else's developments, but if you really want to stand out, you have to be innovative. Show the market that you know your stuff, and try to always think one step ahead of your competitors. Your credibility and others' respect for you will soar.

## Build your own credibility

If you want to be a successful entrepreneur, you have to "bring your own chair to the table." By definition, being an entrepreneur means that you have what it takes to make your presence known and the ability to demonstrate your worth to others. But you have to establish that yourself. It always helps to get an introduction, but you have to take over from there. Don't rely on riding someone else's coattails to get you there.

I have learned over the years that others will determine your worth, but in order for that value to be seen, people have to have confidence in you. You build confidence and credibility by showing people that you have what it takes both personally and professionally. That means, for example, that if you think you should attend a meeting that your boss or supervisor is involved in, you should not automatically assume your boss has to bring you along. There will be times when the boss doesn't feel you can add any value to the meeting. In such cases, if you disagree, you have to make your own arrangements. If you want to be seen as having value, set up your own meetings, establish your own relationships and work to build your own network of contacts, connections and opportunities.

## Sometimes, give without expecting anything in return

It's a good idea, even though it seems counterintuitive, to spend time on activities that do not immediately generate revenues. If you take the time to build up your network and cultivate partners, you will find that they will contribute to making new opportunities and generate more revenue and value for your business down the road. One way to build credibility is to give to someone else without expecting something in return—to give for the sake of helping someone else. There is a saying: "What you give, you will get back tenfold."

## Share the bad news as well as the good

Many people tend to share only the good news with stakeholders or partners, and withhold the bad. But what's worse than hearing bad news is hearing it when it's too late. By sharing the good *and* the bad, you are showing that, regardless of the situation, you will be honest and will look for support. No one can help you solve a problem if they don't know it exists.

## Be confident

When speaking about your products or services, be confident in your delivery and your subject. If you come across as knowing what you are talking about, your audience will have confidence in you, and that will begin to develop your credibility.

## Don't compromise your ethics

You will earn and keep a reputation as a reliable and trustworthy businessperson more easily if you have shown by your actions that you have solid ethical principles. I have been surprised at how often in business one comes across someone who will ask you for a kickback. A company representative will tell you that, with a little extra money for themselves—not for their company—they are willing to help you complete whatever transaction it is you are trying to close with their employer. Somehow, you have to reject this kind of unethical arrangement without compromising either your ethics or your good relationship with the other company. The trick is to put the issue back in the lap of the person requesting the kickback. My answer, every time, is to tell the rep that if their company agrees to their getting an additional payment, I am open to further discussions. Of course, no self-respecting company would agree to such an arrangement, so the talk ends there.

## Credibility brings its own rewards

During the development of my businesses, I have had a hard climb gaining trust and building credibility, not only in my business skills, but in my personal worth as well. But having earned the trust and built the credibility, I have often noticed their positive effects.

# A Little Psychology

Understanding your "target" (the person you are about to leverage in trying to get new business opportunities) is critical to tapping into the power of leverage. Being able to read people is an important component in determining how best to develop an appropriate strategy.

When I first set out to try to get licensors to agree to give me the rights to products that other companies had in their contracts, I didn't really know how to go about it. I knew that in order to leverage something you want from another party, you had to be able to read them and understand how they operate in order to create a win-win scenario. The challenge was to actually do the reading, to find out the right buttons to press. What was it that motivated Disney, Nickelodeon, Marvel, Warner Brothers and the other entertainment companies? Over time, I learned that, by listening carefully to their questions and concerns, watching their body language at critical moments, and asking strategic questions in order to find out potential problems, I was able to discover some of the key factors driving these companies and some of the key differences among them.

Money, of course, was a huge motivation, but I started to notice it wasn't all about money. Yes, they wanted their partners to sell their products and make them money, but they also wanted to make sure that the end-users were satisfied with the quality of the products, that the retailers were happy with the delivery and relationships with us, and that the products being developed were innovative and well manufactured. When I started to work with Disney, I noticed how loyal they were to their partners. (This made me even more confident that I had made the right decision in going after the entertainment companies.) Disney wanted to make sure that their partnerships would lead to long-term revenue streams, so if they were going to take the risk of upsetting their other partners, it would be based on facts, potential results and commitments to their long-term goals. That was one of the main reasons why they worked closely with us to ensure our plans would come to fruition. Nickelodeon, on the other hand, seemed to be mostly focused on revenues at the time when I approached them and never required us to provide detailed marketing plans or growth strategies. Marvel was only really concerned about their other partners' reactions, until I mentioned that Disney had just given us the rights. Then they looked at us more seriously.

Of course, making the case for giving us these rights was a little more complicated than just mentioning the name of the other company we were working with. I still had to convince them that giving us the rights to their product lines was the smart choice. In order to do that, as is often the case in business dealings, I had to use some basic business psychology. I had to play a game with them. Just letting them know about the opportunity and how we could work together wouldn't be enough. I had to show them what we were doing with other licensors, let them see that we were focusing on a market they were not strong in, and let them know their competing licensors were locking up key retail shelf space. I had to convince them that the risk lay in *not* working with us.

If they were still hesitant, I would focus on going after smaller product lines or even a single product. I had noticed that **when I asked for one product, these companies were more willing**

**Understand points of interest to leverage**

**to listen because their risk was much more limited than it would be with a whole category of products**. So that's what I did: I asked for one product, and when I got it, I would ask for another product, and so forth. By the end, I had so many product lines that it was as though I had asked for the whole category. Instead, I had leveraged one item at a time in order to get another—a good example of starting small in order, over time, to become big.

One of the main goals in these kinds of negotiations was to get the other party to see how easy and low-risk it would be to work with us, as well as how many opportunities we could bring to them. They first needed to get over their fears of working with my company and, by making them feel that they were gaining much more than they were giving up, we were building up our collateral to go after larger opportunities down the road.

When I was negotiating for the larger opportunities, I noticed that Disney would only give us the rights when they saw that a major customer wanted the product from us. This meant that I had to target my customers first, meet with them and propose my new lines, letting them know that we did not have the rights, but if they were interested, I could make it happen. If they showed interest, I would ask them to send me an email indicating their level of interest, and in some cases I would help them write the email. Then, the buyer would send me the email and I in turn would forward it to my account manager, attaching an example of what the product would look like.

This was the game I had to play because the account managers would only move forward if they saw a real opportunity. This was a little more challenging in the United States than elsewhere because of the size of the market, but it still worked from time to time. I had to stage an opportunity and plant the seed because I knew that just my saying that I could get a major customer would not be enough to satisfy Disney. **By finding out their real needs, I was able to work out ways to meet them and thus succeed in getting more rights.**

**Be able to find a solution**

# Accidentally on Purpose

Establishing good, strong relationships with key people, outside the office as well as within, is an effective way to build credibility and can be critical to the success of your business. Such relationships take time and patience to build and, sometimes, extraordinary measures are required too. Over the years, I have adopted my own strategy for developing and fostering relationships with leading entertainment companies: I arranged to be in the right place at the right time while making it look like a coincidence.

Solid relationships with key people are critical to the success of your business or idea, but they are not always easy to achieve. Relationships are established over time; you can't force them on people. They certainly can't be built through electronic communications alone. It is important to interact face to face, to go out of your way to be involved with the other person in more than just business situations, if that is reasonably possible. In most instances it *is* possible, because, for the most part, people are looking to connect with others in more meaningful ways.

In order to establish these face-to-face connections, you will need to overcome, or at least control, any feelings of intimidation you may have in the presence of high-level industry people. When I first started working with large companies like Disney, I would get really nervous about our upcoming meetings. It wasn't the presentation that scared me; I had confidence in my product, in what I had to deliver and, to a great extent, in myself. But still I felt intimidated. These were senior personnel used to dealing regularly with industry leaders and heads of major corporations. At one time, I could hardly even dream of being in the same room with people of their stature.

But with time and experience, I came to terms with these insecurities. My determination to succeed pushed me to see that, ultimately, people are just people, regardless of their status. Yes, some people have more accomplishments, better connections and more experience in business, but these things don't make them superior or scary. People are different, and we all bring our own strengths to the table.

## People are people and what makes them different from you and me are their experiences. Don't be afraid to approach them.

As I overcame my feelings of intimidation and began to work on establishing strong relationships with key industry people, I came to realize that, for some, business isn't everything. Money isn't everything. I used to think that if I offered someone a win-win proposal, they would have no reason whatsoever not to jump at the opportunity. I was surprised to discover that, with some companies, loyalty is more powerful than money. This was true with some of the entertainment companies I worked with. When I was dealing with prospective buyers, I would use every incentive I could come up with to try to convince them that we were the ones they should sign on with. For some, nothing would work—not even reducing prices, increasing value or customizing products. They already had a great relationship with another supplier that they weren't willing to jeopardize, no matter the price.

Even the buyers at companies who are known for their low prices, like Walmart, would pass over my company in order to stay loyal to a more expensive supplier with whom they had an established relationship. I met with the Walmart buyer numerous times, and even once with a Disney representative at my side. But even though we had better designs, a larger selection and better pricing, the buyer did not want to purchase our licensed products because she didn't want to rock the boat with Hallmark. How could I compete with this? I came to the conclusion that I just had to sell my products everywhere else. I also learned from this that having the best product means nothing if you don't have a well-developed relationship with your prospective buyer.

Over the years, I have adopted my own strategy for developing and fostering relationships with key individuals at leading entertainment companies. I follow three simple rules:

- Be visible so that the company you are trying to connect with knows you are around and "top of mind."
- Be helpful whenever possible.
- Be supportive without expecting anything in return.

Of these three, one of the most effective, and one that I have used several times, is the first. Sometimes, being in the right place at the right time by design rather than by chance is a useful strategy for building relationships that move beyond the office walls.

Conferences, trade shows and other industry events present perfect opportunities for you to make yourself visible. When I first started my business, I would travel to these events in search of key people I wanted to work with, and I would walk around nonchalantly. Instead of watching the booths, however, I watched the crowds. When I saw someone I considered important, I'd put myself in their direct path so that we would "accidentally" run into one another. It's a bit nerve-wracking, but it is often worth it. A pleasant, casual greeting with an industry professional opens the door to more conversations later on, and perhaps even an invitation to an after-event, dinner or party. Such invitations are the entrance to their inner circle. Sometimes, I would merely pass by people I wanted to know better, and I would smile at them. They didn't know who I was, but that didn't matter, because all I wanted was for them to see me, so that when we crossed paths again, they would recall having seen me before in a business setting. **I am a patient person when I am working to build relationships.**

Be patient

Trying to be visible in major cities like Las Vegas or New York can be challenging because there are just so many places people can end up after a conference. How do you find the right spot to bump into the key people you want to meet? As is often the case, some problems call for a little extra, and perhaps a little unusual, effort. To try to arrange a "chance" meeting with the Disney people, my brother and I would spend hours walking from hotel to hotel, peeking into bars and restaurants and pacing through lobbies in the hope of stumbling upon that elusive needle in the haystack—a sighting of another company's reps. Some nights, we never did, but other times (more often than you might expect), we would run into someone who would let slip where the Disney group was staying. **When this happened, we would jump in a cab and rush to the hotel as fast as we could, then park ourselves in the hotel bar and wait.**

React quickly

One time in Las Vegas we waited hours, thinking we had wasted our night, until finally two bigwigs from the Disney creative team walked in and one of them said, "Hey Brad, how are you doing? We've been seeing you guys everywhere lately." That was pretty much it for that meeting, but that was okay with me because they had seen us and we had had a conversation, however brief. Despite the sore feet, the expended energy and hours of walking, we had found a little more exposure for ourselves.

The Disney executive was right: they *had* been seeing us everywhere. At the time, I passed it off as coincidence, but a month before that, my brother and I had hung out with the entire Disney team at a New York City hotel restaurant. As you might have guessed, we had put in a lot of effort earlier that evening to figure out where they were staying and had spent most of the night waiting for them in that rooftop restaurant. After we had nursed our rather expensive drinks for a couple of hours, the Disney people started trickling in. In a short while, about 20 of them, ranging from junior to senior executives, had arrived and were filling in the tables around my brother and me. We actually knew a couple of people in their group, and they invited us to join their table, where the drinks were now free and where we spent the next several hours together talking about anything and everything. The night continued onwards and outwards from bar to bar, where we continued to build out personal connections.

I felt as though we had struck gold that night, and in a way we had. That encounter helped them put a human face on their new, smaller partners and, undoubtedly, helped make our budding business relationship stronger. These connections would lead to even more business in the years to come.

# The Art of Networking

Most business experts will tell you that it takes five years of being in business before your chance of survival increases significantly. Until I entered the world of business, I never understood why. As my experience grew and I gradually learned more about the business world, there came a point when I realized that it takes about five years to build up a stable network of contacts, customers and partners. Each person you know can add to your credibility, revenue and strategic alliances. Networking creates buzz around you and your business, while helping to increase your chance of greater revenue, credibility and opportunity. The more you network, the smaller your world becomes. And the information and contacts you gain from networking can sometimes be even more useful as time goes on. When I started my second business, it grew and became successful much more quickly than the first. One of the main reasons for this was the fact that I had a large network to engage right from the start.

## The more people in your field you connect with, the faster you will reach success

If you have survived the hardships of your first year, you have probably met some competitors, prospective customers and manufacturers. Despite all that, you're still relatively new. You have been spending all your time and energy trying to get noticed, trying to secure meetings and trying to bring in revenue. Most likely, things have not gone the way you thought they would. Maybe you have even reached some kind of crisis. Many people decide at this point to move back into the regular workforce, chalking up their experience as an entrepreneur as a lesson of life. And if that's your decision, there is nothing wrong with reverting back to a nine-to-five paycheque. Being self-employed is not for everyone, and it is certainly not easy.

If you do not go that route, you will soon have year two in the books. By now, you will have contacted even more prospective customers and developed even more relationships; your network is increasing. As you make more contacts and build new relationships, you are continually learning how to develop your business, and successes start to build. You make even more sales here and there, and by year three, more and more things start to happen. The longer you're in business, the more your achievements accumulate. Over time, your network will become so large that you might even be considered an expert in your field.

## Your connections put trust in you when they give you their contact info. Value it and safeguard it from those who might use it for the wrong reasons.

Since I started my first business, I have built up a significant number of contacts and relationships. I have kept all my business cards, all my emails, databases and details around my relationships so that one day, if I needed them, they would be at my fingertips. I keep my contacts very close to me and will not share them with others unless I know it would add benefit to my contacts. Selling off your network information is not a smart thing to do. It takes considerable time and effort to gain the confidence of the people and companies contained in it. The last thing you want to do is jeopardize this. I have been approached by many people over the years, both those close to me and strangers, asking if they could get access to my relationships with the entertainment companies, manufacturers, retailers, investors and distribution partners. I think that out of all the requests I have had, I have given only one or two introductions.

As I was developing my business, I networked whenever and wherever I could. I would go to events, listen to the keynote speakers and seek them out afterward in order to introduce myself and ask for a business card. Collecting business cards from industry professionals became a sort of hobby for me; it was proof that we had actually met, and I would leverage it when I spoke with someone else—but only when appropriate, of course. If, for example,

I was talking with someone who mentioned a company they had been trying to work with, a company one of whose representatives or managers I had met, I would pull out my book with the business cards stapled to it, alongside notes to my conversation. They would immediately look at the card and then comment on my book and how organized I was. This would also add to my credibility, because they would see that I had met a lot of other people too. Even if these individuals weren't in their field, the presence of the cards showed that I networked quite a bit.

The following are a few simple tips I've gathered from my own networking experience of making new contacts:

## Ask personal questions about what they like, how they got into their field, where they are from

Gently probing questions, so long as they are not too personal, will lead you to details that you might be able to relate to. It is important to try to connect with people. Don't simply ask yes-or-no questions, because those won't lead to further conversation. For example, "Do you like what you do?" usually elicits only a quick yes or no in response, but "What do you like about your work?" is likely to produce a longer response, allowing an opportunity for the development of a fuller dialogue.

## Be genuine and stay focused on the person you are talking with

Don't worry about anyone else in the room. People can tell when you are not being real, and if they see you looking around or over their shoulder, they will suspect that you are not really interested in talking with them. Good networking means being engaged and showing that you are genuinely interested in what the other person has to say.

## If you see an opportunity to help the person you are talking to, offer to help and don`t worry about whether you are going to get something in return

If you give, you will get back. Keep thinking this way and it will have a positive impact. It may not happen right away, but in my experience, over time it will. One form of helping that I have engaged in is what I call the "last man standing" approach. Over

Give without
expecting

the years, I attended many events hosted by Disney, and **after the main activity was finished I would stay behind and help the team clean up**. Taking down a booth, cleaning up garbage, etc., provides an excellent opportunity for conversation and relationship building, especially if you're not someone they know much about yet.

Always ask for a business card, and if they don't have one, ask if you can write down their details. Handing them your business card is no substitute for getting contact information, as you may never hear from that person again and, if you don't have their information, you can never reconnect.

Write the details about your conversation on the back of the card or in a notebook afterwards. Don't write the notes in front of the person because you want it to seem as if you are enjoying a conversation, not conducting an interview. The less you can make it seem like a business meeting, the more likely you will connect on a personal level.

Follow up later and remind them of the conversation. This is why you take notes afterwards. Shortly after making a new contact, send them an email saying something like: "Hi, it's John Doe. It was great meeting you at the show. I would love to talk more with you about... By the way, here is the information I mentioned I was going to provide you about the person you asked about..." By doing this, you are hoping to make a positive connection and to stand out from all the other people at the event. Someone might not always be the right contact for exactly what you need, but they might know someone who is.

Networking is easy for some people, but not for everyone. Each time I start to network I become nervous, but that can be expected because I am about to introduce myself to new people. It reminds me of when I was a child, trying to make a new friend and finding it difficult because I was afraid of being rejected. In business, the feeling is much the same and not much easier. But, as with most things in business, you can learn to improve your networking skills, and these can help a great deal in bringing your company success.

# Learning to Talk Less and Listen More

> If you listen more than you talk, you will be better able to hear what someone else is looking for from you. From what you learn in this way, you should be able to meet or exceed their expectations.

I am a talker. This is a trait I have had to work on as I've built my businesses, and am still working on. I know I should talk less and listen more, but my passion sometimes overwhelms my ability to effectively listen. When I would attend meetings with one of my previous business advisors (he later became a board member), he would have a signal for me that would indicate that I was talking too much. He would move his hand slowly up to his neck and make a slight scissor motion that indicated for me to cut the conversation. Sometimes it would work, and other times I kept going to make sure I got my message heard.

Being able to talk a lot can be a good quality when you're trying to get your message across, **but besides interfering with your listening, it can also cause you to reveal too much**. Obviously this can be a real problem if you are the one doing the revealing, but it can be a good thing if it's the other person who is giving the extra information. In those cases, by all means let them talk. Talkers, in their willingness to give more information than you asked for, will often reveal information that you can later use to your benefit.

Don't overshare

With effort, over the past couple of years, I have become a much better listener, and this has enabled me to pick up on more opportunities I would likely have missed before. In one instance I recall, I was in a meeting with the Ontario Lottery Group, trying to sell them on what my company, iPal, does. After I gave my pitch, I asked them to talk about what their overall learning objectives were, and I listened carefully to their answer. When they mentioned some of their challenges, I took note of them and any ideas that came to me on how we could help solve their problems.

Right after the meeting ended, I chatted to them about some of their issues and my ideas on how we could probably help them. They seemed intrigued with the ideas, and a couple of months later I was asked to complete a proposal on one of them. This eventually led to a new contract for us that was completely unrelated to my original presentation.

Often in business, **the ability to be a good listener is as valuable as being a good talker**. Even if patient listening does not come naturally to you, you can learn to develop it.

Be a good listener

# Confidence—with a Dash of Humility

Most people enjoy being around confident people. They give off a positive aura that leads in turn to positive responses and actions. Confidence can help a great deal in building credibility in business. It is also important that it be mixed with a bit of humility in order to avoid crossing the line into arrogance.

Having confidence in what you are saying and doing, and showing it, is an important factor in establishing personal and business credibility. Exhibiting confidence reassures people that you know what you are doing and that they can trust you. With that reassurance, they are more likely to take you seriously and want to continue working with you. Confidence is one of the key traits that people look for in a leader, and showing leadership qualities is one of the distinguishing features of successful entrepreneurs.

Some people are confident by nature, but many are not. For those in the latter category, confidence can be developed. I was very insecure in high school and kept to myself all the time. I didn't speak out in class or volunteer for any event that would put me front and centre. Today, this is not the case. I forced myself to be a leader, forced myself to do things that would gradually increase my confidence.

I wanted to do things, wanted to stand out, so I realized I needed to get out of my shell. To this day, I still get nervous when I am going to speak in front of people, but I have learned to control this. The trick to coming out of that shell is to push yourself, put yourself in situations where you have to take on bigger challenges. These are risky situations and may cause you embarrassment, but if you truly are determined you will have some success in those situations. As with building a business, small success soon leads to a little more success and, in time, to full confidence.

## Being a successful entrepreneur means being out there. It requires that you stand out from the rest in a crowd!

When I was younger, I found it extremely difficult to be put on the spot for public speaking or some other spotlight-type activity. Later, because I wanted to change that, I put myself in positions that forced me to be at the centre of attention, and to speak out amongst large groups. When I won a competitive posting to the job of program manager at the Bank of Canada, for example, one of my responsibilities was to chair what we called the "war room." This was where all the managers and team leads would come together every morning for 15 minutes to walk through issues, risks and updates. I was responsible for ensuring that everyone kept on track during these sessions. My boss was the type of person who ruled by fear, so when he expected you to keep everyone on track, you would do it—otherwise he would embarrass you in front of everyone. All the section representatives were given exactly the same amount of time—two minutes each—to speak about their own section, and I was the person assigned to cut them off at the two-minute mark, no matter what.

Of course, all of these people were managers, so cutting them off gave me a sort of authority for those 15 minutes. There were occasions when some people would continue to talk and I would be forced to step in and remind them of the time limit. Given my general lack of confidence, this was not an easy task for me. When I first started doing it, I was always nervous, with butterflies filling my stomach and the palms of my hands getting sweaty as I watched the clock creeping towards the two-minute mark, knowing that I would have to step in and say something soon. When I first took on the position in this department, my job did not include this particular responsibility, but I am glad it did because it forced me to step out of my shell and be the centre of attention for a brief period every day.

There is no doubt that having the confidence to speak in front of others can be an asset when you are trying to build a business. Recently in my second business, iPal Interactive Learning, I needed to gain credibility in the industry, so I wrote and submitted a proposal to speak in November 2010 at the largest education conference in Canada, the Canadian Society of Training and Development (CSTD) conference. A couple months after I submitted my proposal, I received an email from the CSTD stating that the committee loved my topic and wanted to know if I could speak for an hour and a half at the conference. That's a long time to be speaking, but I agreed anyway. My stomach started to turn with nervousness, even though the conference was almost a year away, and I wondered what I had agreed to. (Even as I recall and write about this now, my stomach is in knots. That goes to tell you how serious the anxiety can get.)

## Public speaking provides a level of credibility that can help advance your business much faster. Take the plunge.

Despite those initial feelings, I was very excited about this opportunity. I thought about the longer term. I knew this would provide me with several things to use as leverage in the future. I could tell people that I had been selected to speak at Canada's largest educational conference, a sure indication that I must know what I'm talking about. There would be good networking opportunities. But even more important, by digging down and

drawing on my inner strength and giving this address, I would be building up my confidence. This, in turn, would contribute to increased credibility.

As I gained confidence in myself, it started to show when I spoke. Even when I did not know the subject very well, or wasn't really sure about the answer to a question, it came across that I had something useful to say because I spoke with confidence. But I would never imply that I knew everything. I would give my opinion, and that was it. Some would take my thoughts as factual or useful, while others might seriously question them. Regardless of how the conversation went, I would try to be open-minded and, if I sensed that the other person was knowledgeable on the subject under discussion, I would take that as an opportunity to learn something new. If the other person didn't know the subject well, no harm was done. We all have our thoughts, theories and opinions. Being able to share them, whether we are right or wrong, will generally be a positive thing.

Of course, in giving your thoughts or answering a question, **you have to be careful that you don't cross the line into totally fabricating a wild and obviously unbelievable answer**. That would give you a different reputation—and not a very positive one. There are times when you have to come right out and say, "I don't know." That, too, can be taken as an expression of confidence.

**Don't ever exaggerate or embellish**

Another line to avoid crossing is the fine one that separates strong, healthy confidence from arrogance. There is a big difference between the two, and the latter is more likely to hinder the building of credibility than aid it. A dash of humility mixed with your confidence will keep you on the more likeable and effective side of that line.

This is good advice that can be applied to different situations. Like any loving dad, I have often told my young daughters, Kloé and Alexandra, how pretty they are. For some time, on each occasion that I said this to the older one, Alexandra, she would reply, "Yeah, I know." This response, even for a child, comes down on the arrogant side of that line, so I had to teach her the importance of humility when compliments are given. Now she replies, "Thank you."

You will sometimes hear it said that "Business is business and it is nothing personal," but I do not find that to be true.

There is a personal aspect to most business activities, because you are dealing with people and their emotions. Because of that, it is important that you try to carry yourself in a manner that will earn their respect and admiration. **Humility interwoven with your confidence is also important in getting people to connect with you on a personal level.** If they sense that you are bragging or behaving as though you are better than they are, there is a good chance you will lose them. Even if you know you're doing well, there's no need to tell everyone

**Stay humble**

about it in long, boastful detail. People want to work with others who are easy-going, who show a little humility and make them feel important and equal. If you come across as thinking you are better than others, you will never be able to really connect with them personally and professionally.

Over the years, I have worked with a couple of people who felt the need to list all their accomplishments and successes during meetings and discussions. This is very off-putting. No one likes a braggart, and it doesn't take long for one's interest in what these kinds of people have to say to turn into annoyance with them. They probably don't realize that, even though they're trying so hard to seem confident and in control, they actually come across as being insecure. It is much better to let people see you for who you are instead of boasting about what you've done. Your self-confidence says more than words ever could, and others will be able to see your success in your confident demeanour. People can read confidence in your body language, and hear it in the excitement and positivity in your voice. Unlike overconfidence and arrogance, which turn people off, these are infectious qualities that will cause others to feel excited and positive too.

# 9

## Under New Management

EXPERIENCED A VARIETY OF DIFFERENT EMOTIONS when I first started hiring staff. I was excited because I was in a position to hire people, but at the same time I felt I was losing my company. Having to delegate did not come easily. I was so used to doing things my way that when other people started to contribute, it bothered me that their way often wasn't mine. Over time, however, I learned to trust them. After all, that is what they were being hired for.

# Letting Go

> It is important to trust in the people you have hired and to have confidence that they will do a good job when they are assigned work to do. People who start a business sometimes have a hard time letting go and sharing responsibility. Once you do, you will be able to advance your business much faster and more efficiently.

Sometimes, the biggest obstacle to progress is you. I have been there! As I built my first business, I became more and more controlling. It's not that I was an overbearing control freak (at least I hope not), but I just felt the need to do everything myself. I would get home late and spend hours more developing programs and completing tasks that I was paying people to do for me during the day. I felt as though if I weren't a part of everything that was going on in my company, it wouldn't be done right. I felt that, if I took a step back, I would be replacing myself with employees who might not have what it took to represent my vision and ideas. "Let me do my job!" they would tell me, over and over. It took years before I finally listened, but I'm so glad I did.

Once your company gets to a certain size, doing everything yourself becomes impossible. As my business started to really take shape, I came to realize that if I wanted it to truly develop into the business I envisioned, I would have to learn to trust my people and to let go. **I came to see that, if I stepped back and let my**

**employees do the job, they wouldn't be replacing me but rather supporting me.** I saw that not allowing my employees to do their jobs would not only hold me back, it would be unfair to them. When I finally let go, my staff became an extension of my own efforts, helping me advance to levels I could never have reached on my own. That was when I understood the true meaning of the word "team."

Be able to delegate

As a result of giving my team control, they were empowered to do more and take on responsibility for their work. This empowerment ensured that they took pride in what they did, and this in turn improved the results for my clients. In addition, I gained their respect because I trusted them, and they gained my confidence because they were proving to me that they could do the work. My team has become more than just employees now. As a result of this change in my leadership style, not one employee under my management over my years as a boss has quit, something I am very proud of.

> ## Employees are only as good as they are allowed to be. If you give them your trust they can be great. If you give them your control, they can become disenchanted.

When you're working towards a goal, you have to use all the available resources in the best way that you can. Clearly, some of your most important resources are your own employees. When I stopped controlling every little detail, I became a stronger leader and manager. My results and free time increased. I could focus my energies on issues that mattered more to me, such as enhancing productivity, increasing revenue and developing new partnerships instead of daily operational duties. Being the boss doesn't mean having your hands in everything; rather, it means leading and encouraging the development of your ideas through the team's abilities and creativity.

Now I try to instil this wisdom into my management team. Like me, some of those promoted from worker to leader are finding the transition a real challenge. Learning the many benefits of letting go and delegating is never easy.

# The Boss Is an Employee of the Workers

Good, effective managers work to ensure that their staff feel a part of a team, and that they are respected, appreciated and, collectively, a valuable asset to the business. They lead by example, by working with their employees and not, as is the case with some bosses, by fear.

Be a team player

A good boss is **not simply a manager or leader, but also a good team player**. A manager makes demands, lays out constraints and puts pressure on employees to perform; a leader will guide, support and encourage in order to get the best from employees. But it shouldn't end there. In order to fully utilize employees' capabilities, the boss needs to move beyond the managerial position and become a team player, showing leadership through trust, support and confidence in the team. As a boss who leads by example, you show your employees that you are willing to work alongside them and do whatever they do.

No task is beneath a good boss when it comes to pitching in to help out their staff. When they see that their staff is stressed or being drowned with work, they will step in, without needing to be asked, and help wherever they can. They will take on some of their employees' responsibilities if need be, so that they can help them get out of the weeds. In addition to working alongside and assisting their staff, effective bosses sometimes do little extras for them to let them know that they are appreciated.

There have been many times when I have noticed that members of my staff have worked late. To acknowledge their efforts and indicate my appreciation, I sometimes send them an email telling them to take an extra day off as compensation for the extra effort. I wouldn't do this all the time, as it would become expected, but as an occasional gesture it lets the staff know you notice and care. At other times, I have walked into the design area and told **the employees that I was taking them all to see a movie that afternoon**. These unexpected gestures show the staff that I appreciate them and that I am willing to do what it takes to make sure that they feel a valuable part of the business.

Show unexpected appreciation

Respected and effective leaders work side by side with their employees when they can, to help establish a team mindset and ensure that the team feels like a valued asset to the company. I would never ask my staff to do something I am not prepared to do myself. Good leadership means treating people with loyalty and respect, and in return earning their loyalty and respect. You catch more flies with honey than with vinegar. If you treat people fairly, they will more often than not return the favour. They will go the extra mile, doing things like staying late on occasion without having to be asked, when they understand what needs to get done and feel that they have a responsible role to play.

At the other extreme from the good bosses are the managers who use vinegar instead of honey, the ones who rule by fear. When I worked for the Bank of Canada, I had such a boss. He would frequently belittle his staff in an attempt to shame them into not making mistakes. Every day, he would scream at us and make demeaning comments about our intelligence or some other characteristic in front of everyone. I suspect he did this because he had no real leadership skills, and he must have thought that if he scared people they would do exactly what he wanted. He was abusive, and what made it worse was that he seemed to enjoy it. He loved the control, and he wanted everyone to know that they were below him. I don't think one person ever voluntarily stayed after hours to help him out when he needed it. To this day, I cannot understand how he achieved a managerial role in this department.

I did note, however, that after the division was outsourced, he was one of the first to be let go.

Despite all the pain this boss caused me during my time there, he did teach me one valuable lesson. His behaviour made me realize the dangers that can come from having power over others. I promised myself that if I ever had staff reporting to me, I would never treat them as he treated us.

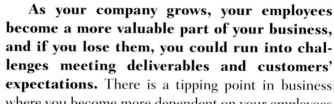

Keep your team

**As your company grows, your employees become a more valuable part of your business, and if you lose them, you could run into challenges meeting deliverables and customers' expectations.** There is a tipping point in business where you become more dependent on your employees than they are on you. The boss becomes the employee, so to speak. A critical mass of customers, infrastructure and so forth creates a stable environment that enables the business to run seamlessly. This does not mean that you are no longer required, but it does mean that your employees' worth in the company might have increased to the point where their leaving could create issues. For example, when you have an employee who works with all your key customers and builds up personal relationships with them, their departure could jeopardize those relationships. As an employer, it is wise to always treat your workers fairly, making sure they are happy, involved, appreciated and respected. Once you reach this tipping point, this becomes even more important.

Treating people fairly and respectfully, of course, is wise in most business situations, not just in employer-employee relationships. Generally speaking, you will increase your chances of getting that purchase order or introduction you want by showing patience and respect towards the other party rather than being rude with them. Whether in a business office, a restaurant or a golf club, people at all levels of employment, by and large, are entitled to basic appreciation and respect for their work.

# Family and Friends as Employees

Family and friends can be valuable to a business in its start-up phase, but as the business grows and gains more employees, they can create special challenges for the boss. These require careful managing in order to head off negative effects on the workplace. In a developed business, the best policy is not to hire family members or friends.

In developing a successful business, one of your important jobs will be learning how to effectively lead and work with employees. When some of these employees are friends and members of your family, there are added challenges you have to address.

At the beginning of my business and throughout its development, I regularly had family and friends working for me. In some cases, the friends were friends prior to working for me; in others, the friendship developed after they had become my employees. It was very beneficial to have these people involved at the beginning when I needed that kind of support. When people are close to you, they may be willing to come through for you in difficult times—by stepping up, for example, to assist when finances are low.

As my business started to grow in size and complexity, however, with an increased employee base, multiple business partners and so forth, the dynamics affecting the people close to me became more complicated. Because we were close, some family and friends had acquired a sense of entitlement. This would become apparent when they questioned, second-guessed or openly challenged my decisions. In some cases, if I did not move ahead with their recommendations, they would suggest that I wasn't taking them seriously and argue with me. The worst cases occurred when they challenged my decisions in front of other employees or partners. Having someone, anyone—family, friends or other employees—behave like this creates an awkward situation that forces you to take action or risk

**Relationship is business**

losing the respect of your other employees. As a boss, you are required to address this behaviour and, unfortunately, put these people in their place. **Even though they may be close to you personally, business is business, and you expect employees to respect your decisions regardless of personal relationships.** If employees disagree with a decision, they should discuss the matter only in private. By raising it and arguing about it in front of others, they give the false impression that they have decision-making responsibilities that, in reality, only the boss has.

When these situations arose, I would always listen to the concerns being raised, but I would still make the decision that I thought was best for my company. At the end of the day, I had the most to lose, the most vested and the most responsibility for the business's successes.

## As a boss, being friendly is important, but be aware of the challenges when becoming friends

There are other ways in which family members as employees can be awkward. There have been occasions, for example, when other employees complained to me about family members or friends of mine whom I had hired. In some cases, this was not easy for them to do. They were concerned that I would either do nothing or let the person they were complaining about go. Some complaints that I received were quite serious—serious enough to disrupt productivity and cause my other staff to feel unimportant and underappreciated. The implied accusation was that family and friends had been hired because of who they were and not necessarily because of their skills. This charge is probably justified when you first start your business, because you need the support of people who will work either cheaply or for free—i.e., family or friends—at a time when you cannot afford full-time employees.

But when it comes to the survival of your business, you need to put the greater good above personal needs and address these issues as they come up. In these circumstances, I kept the employees' complaints confidential and never mentioned them to my family or friends. These are obviously tough conversations to have, but they are needed. An employer needs to be able to have firm and honest discussions with employees when the circumstances demand it, without the fear of ruining their personal relationships.

Family members and friends were valuable to my business in the early going. Over time, however, I have come to the conclusion that with a more developed business the best policy is not to hire people with whom you are personally close. With the exception of my wife, I now stick firmly to this policy. My wife is the only family member I have worked with who fully understands the difference between work and personal life. When I ask her to do something at work, she does it. She will, like any other of my employees, suggest ways to make improvements, but she understands and respects her role and her position within the company. She is the exception. Generally speaking, I have found that family members and friends either do not understand or do not respect the boundaries between close personal relationships and employee status. They are less likely to take orders without questioning, and they find it difficult, if not impossible, to put aside the many personal aspects of the relationship.

For me as the boss, there were extra pressures brought on by the family/friend-employer dynamic. I would not hesitate to discipline or terminate my other employees if needed. When it came to family members and friends, I would not act so quickly. I would think about it, spending more time weighing the pros and cons and trying to figure out how I could talk with them, tiptoeing around the situation so that they would not be upset. That is not fair to the employer, the staff or, in the end, the family members and friends.

When I promote my staff into managerial roles, I always have a conversation with them about friendships in the workplace. I mention the challenges I have faced in the past and let them know that you can be friendly with the people who report to you, but cannot become friends. There needs to be a separation between manager and employee, and it is important that the line not be crossed in order to avoid unnecessary difficulty with effective disciplining later, should it be required.

One of my newly promoted design managers asked me if she could hire her younger brother to work as a designer. He was studying in the multimedia field at a local college and would normally have been the perfect candidate, but, since he was a member of her family and she would be his boss, I had reservations. She understood those, but believed that in this case it would not be an issue. I always try to respect the decisions of my management team, so I said she could decide this one on her own. She hired her brother, which I accepted, with the understanding that I would speak with him about my rules regarding working with family.

There are always exceptions to a rule

**I told him that it was against my better judgment to hire him to work under his sister**, but since she thought there would not be any issues, we would go ahead. Knowing that she would never tell me if she were having any work-related issues with her brother, I said I would keep an eye out and not hesitate to step in if I sensed there were problems. Fortunately, there was no need to step in. I was very pleased with their working relationship. In fact, I ended up trying to convince him to stay on when he notified me he was going back to school for his last semester. Even firm manager-employee policies can have a grey area that calls for flexibility.

# A Definite Maybe

An effective boss must be able to able to make decisions and stick by them. Some of the toughest decisions involve letting employees go. In making your decisions, listen to what others have to say and consider their opinions, but in the end, make your own calls. This will show that you are able to lead and take responsibility for your choices.

It goes without saying that, if you are building a company and you are the boss, you often will have to make decisions. Both in the day-to-day routine and in planning for the longer term, decisions need to be made all the time. Sometimes, of course, they are hard to make. If you waver between yes, no and maybe, people will eventually lose confidence in your ability to lead. **It's important to show people that, when you have to do it, you can make the call.** It is also important that you stand by the decisions you make.

Be able to make decisions

The hardest decisions are those that bring bad news, particularly those involving letting employees go. I have found that, no matter how many of these difficult decisions you make over the years, it never gets easy. The hardest ones of all are those involving staff members who are close to you. But even with those, I have found that, if I don't sugar-coat the reasons, people are usually receptive to the decision. It is best, once you have made a decision to let an employee go, not to put off the conversation. Most people I know, or who work for me, tend to delay these talks because they are difficult, but when the decision has been made, you not only owe it to yourself, but to the person being dismissed, to have the conversation.

About a week after I had hired one young man, I asked my team, as I usually do, how he was settling in. I always want to make sure that each employee fits within our work culture and that all are working well together. If there are issues right away, you know it will never work. Even with a proper hiring process, an employee who is not a good fit will sometimes get through.

I was travelling when I called in to my design manager to talk to her about a client when she mentioned some complaints she had heard about the new hire's work and office behaviour. The complaints were serious enough that I knew right away I would have to dismiss him. He was starting to connect with my customers, so I also knew that I would have to inform him of my decision right away, even though I wasn't scheduled to be back in the office for a few more days. I could not have someone who would no longer be working with me being introduced to my customers. My design manager did not want me to terminate his employment until I got back. She was concerned about how he might react, and the fact that he would likely blame her. I emphasized to her the need to act immediately. I called him right away and explained the issues, but never mentioned the employees who had complained about his work and demeanour. I also called my business partner, who was at the office, to make sure the employee was escorted from the building and did not to disrupt other staff.

## Your gut decisions are usually the right ones. It is your mind that talks you out of taking action. Follow your gut feelings.

These decisions are hard to make because there are so many emotions involved. The young man was not very pleased about being let go, but who would be? He asked several times during our conversation if I could give him another chance, but it was too late. The damage had already been done, and besides, if I gave him a second chance, how would I look to my other employees? **I would lose credibility for not sticking with my decision, a decision that was right for the company as a whole.**

Stick to your decisions

# Education and Experience

Having an education is great in helping open doors for you. Once you are through those doors, you must know how to apply what you have learned to get results. If you are not able to do this, education alone will not get you very far. Experience provides you with an understanding of what is required of you in the working world. If you can get both an education *and* experience in your field, you will be that much farther ahead of others.

I have always believed that learning from experience and results achieved is more effective than focusing on theory alone. In my case, by far the greatest part of my learning has come from experience. As I have indicated throughout the book, my business successes were achieved largely because I was able to learn from experience and leverage what I learned from one situation into advancing further.

A while ago, I was working as a professor of project management at Algonquin College in Ottawa, having recently earned my Project Management Professional designation through years of hands-on experience. Before the semester began, I was preparing my course materials and flipping through the textbook that the course coordinator had given me. It was written by two students from an Ivy League university in the United States, and so I was surprised that they didn't seem to know what they were talking about. There were contradictions from one page to the next, and theories tied together using incorrect models and examples. I dug a little deeper and learned that the authors were right out of school with no industry experience whatsoever.

The more I read, the more I realized I could not teach with this text because of the significant discrepancies between their content and that taught by the Project Management Institute, the governing body for project management, also based in the United States. I approached the coordinator and explained my concerns, which, after seeing how many mistakes there were, she quite understood. She said she couldn't understand how the book had been approved for use, but I did. It was written and published by people with credentials, so everyone assumed it must be good and that the authors knew what they were talking about. After this, I decided to write my own materials for the classes, and it worked. I taught using my own materials for several years with great success—primarily, in my view, because they were based on actual experience in the areas being covered. Learning from someone with experience provides an advantage over learning from someone who has never left the classroom, because with the former you are also receiving context. Of course, if you are able to acquire both experience and theory, even better.

I have personally been through many situations where I was denied an interview because I did not have a degree. Whether I was qualified or not did not matter. Judgment about my ability to handle a position was based on my resumé, in particular the degrees that it showed I had or didn't have. Most companies seem to assume that people with post-secondary education must have the skills to do the work. This requirement limits their candidate selection to a level of perceived knowledge only. The reality is that education provides a toolbox for people to use in building up their skills, but when they are required to apply their knowledge, education itself cannot help them. They still have to be self-reliant, hard-working, able to take direction, accept criticism, be able to lead, follow, solve problems and do much more that comes from actual experience outside the classroom.

I have hired several MBAs and engineers over the years. Many of them were great at taking direction, but, when asked to make a decision on their own, would stumble and struggle. When I asked them to do tasks that they considered administrative in nature, I would hear them say things like "This isn't an MBA type of task" or "I am not an admin person." These individuals felt that because they had a degree they should not only be paid more, but also should only do work they considered equal to their perceived status. I have made it a practice to start these employees off at a lower pay level than they thought their education entitled them to, and have told them that they had to prove they could do the job. If they were able to live up to their own perceived value, I would increase their pay to match their qualifications. This way, it was fair to us and to them. Sadly, I have had to terminate the relationships with many of these individuals because they could not work within an entrepreneurial environment and acquire the work-based education to supplement their formal education.

When I am looking to hire people, I don't base my decision on their degrees, but primarily on their experience. If they have a degree without experience and I think they have what it takes, I will take them on at a lower pay level and give them a chance to show what they can do. If they don't have a degree, I have only their experience on which to determine if they are qualified. If they don't have either degree or experience, their chances are slim. With just education, you are required to prove yourself; with just experience, you may not get an audience to be able to prove yourself.

# Building a Culture

Building a business also means having to build a team that includes more than you. The challenge I have always faced is to find the right people for what I am trying to build. Over the years I have had some great successes with this, and also some terrible failures. The successes have been the people who supported my vision, were easy to get along with, communicated freely with me on both the good and the bad and showed the appropriate level of professionalism and respect not only to me, but to others. They trusted in the direction I was taking the company and believed in positivity and forward thinking.

The failures were different. They were the people who might not have agreed with me and the direction I was taking my company, yet they felt entitled to try and change this direction, even though they neither possessed the experience to do so nor had they taken the risks to get the business to where I had brought it. They seemed to feel that if I could do it, it must be easy. Perhaps they had more education than I did; or were older, so they assumed they had more experience; or, because they were specialized, figured they were more skilled.

The challenge in dealing with these employees was that instead of discussing their concerns, interests or opportunities for improvements with me, they would instead do things behind my back in a manner that was more destructive than constructive. What does this say about their values? When things did not go their way, they would complain to their co-workers, to partners and, in some cases, even to my clients. When these behaviours occur, especially within a growing company, the results are miscommunication and confusion that result in mistrust, disloyalty and disrespect. The poisoning of a growing company by employees who are not aligned with the leader's vision and values can be the downfall of the company. I have had to learn this lesson too many times with people who just did not seem to get what I was building. Perhaps that was my fault for not clearly defining where I was taking the company, but for the most part it seemed to go deeper than that. It seemed to be more about a failure to align the company's values with those of the individual.

It can be difficult to find the right people because everyone lies during interviews. Being on one's best behaviour and making sure you provide all the right answers to questions is what will get you the job. When asked to name our three biggest weaknesses, for example, we all give the same type of answer: "Well, that is a tough one. I am not sure if working hard and paying attention to details would be considered a weakness." The consequence of hiring someone on the basis of a misleading interview because a vacancy has to be filled is too often precisely the situation where the company values and the employee's values don't line up. The last time I checked, we all have the ability to be happy and to work in a place that meets our personal needs. We can all make money almost anywhere, but we can't necessarily be happy everywhere.

## Values drive a person's behaviour. Make sure your resources share in the same values to drive your success.

The last round of layoffs that I have had to make was because of this misalignment of employee and company values. Individuals we hired had, during their interviews, led me and my managers to believe their values were aligned with my own and those of the culture we were trying to build. Perhaps they exaggerated their experience as well; I usually assume that most of what candidates say in an interview is not 100 per cent truthful. There are, however, key values that I expect from all I employ. These include being respectful, loyal, honest, result-oriented, positive-thinking, driven, reliable, passionate, considerate and professional. When building my businesses, I never really paid much attention or even knew how to understand what drove another person's actions when they were faced with difficult or challenging situations. The fact is, I never had to think about it before I had difficult employees to deal with. When these people would behave in a manner that was not what I would consider professional or with the best use of judgment, I started to question why they would behave that way. What caused their behaviour, and why did they honestly feel it was okay? I came to realize that it all came down to their basic values.

It is from these negative experiences that I developed a model that would help me better align the right people for my company's culture. You may be wondering why a culture is important. In the end, culture helps shape how your organization is seen in the industry. Here is how the issues surrounding values and behaviour all come together.

There are six factors—four drivers and two contributors—that I have determined make sense in understanding what builds a culture that reflects the values I believe are essential. I am not saying that this is the right approach for everyone, but it sure helped me to understand what I need to look for in the people I hire:

## Drivers:
- Your Values
- Company Values
- Team Behaviour
- Team Actions

## Contributors:
- Your brand
- Industry Impressions

In building a business, it is **your values** that will shape how the company will look and how it will be perceived by the industry in years to come. If you are service-oriented, have a sense of pride in your work and are loyal, patient and compassionate, you may end up being seen in the industry as a customer service–focused company that puts the customer's needs first. This factor also applies to the people you are looking at hiring. They also need to ask themselves the same questions about what is important to them. If, for example, they are more passionate, results-oriented, driven, innovative and forward thinking, they may not be as customer service–focused as you would want them to be. They may be more focused on providing products to as many people as possible and always looking for something better.

**Company values** include the baseline values you want to see in all the people you bring on board. If you want your company to be customer service–oriented, you need to make sure that the values that drive that result are inherent in the people you hire. In building your company culture, you need to transfer your values to the company, because you might not always be around to reinforce them yourself. It can be very difficult to find employees who are exactly aligned with your values; if you define what you believe to be your key values and list them, you will at least be able to ensure you are on the right track.

# Your team should be what you want your company to represent.

When I was forced to come to terms with my values and their significance for the company, I only had to look at my **team behaviour** to truly distinguish the good from the bad. For the most part, my team seemed to behave the same way I would. However, there were a few who seemed to be out of whack to what I regarded as common sense. One instance of conflicting values that could have taken the business right down the toilet—literally!—occurred one day at the office when I was meeting with a client. On the same day, iPal's head office human resources manager was in from Toronto to help me assess some of my staff's capabilities. I was approached by one of my team members about an incident in the washroom. She wanted to let me know that she had found a fake piece of shit on the ledge in our bathroom and had removed it. I found out later that one of our designers was trying to be funny and thought that a day when both a client and our head office's HR manager were on the premises would be the appropriate moment to play a bathroom prank. I would question whether that type of behaviour would ever be appropriate in a business environment, but he thought it was that day. I was lucky that it was one of my staff who found the item—and removed it from the washroom— instead of the client or HR manager.

When I spoke to my staff about what I considered to be proper behaviour, I also mentioned that their **actions** do speak louder than their words. It is easy to say that one believes their behaviours are aligned with a culture, until their actions say otherwise. It is these actions that can really build or break a company. I came to realize that in building a culture, truly understanding a person's behaviours starts with watching their actions.

The values, behaviours and actions of your employees will build up your **brand** and the **industry impressions** of your company. It is these elements that will help continue to build your culture by attracting partners and new recruits who want to be part of your work environment. What your brand represents is what other see in your organization.

Your brand and industry impressions contribute to the type of people who are attracted to your team. When you build your business and it grows, ask yourself what message is being sent to the industry about your work environment, your flexibility or the constraints that affect your employees. If your values are helping you to hire the right people, and the outcomes of their actions are shaping your brand in a positive way, it only makes sense that these factors will help attract more of the kind of people you need.

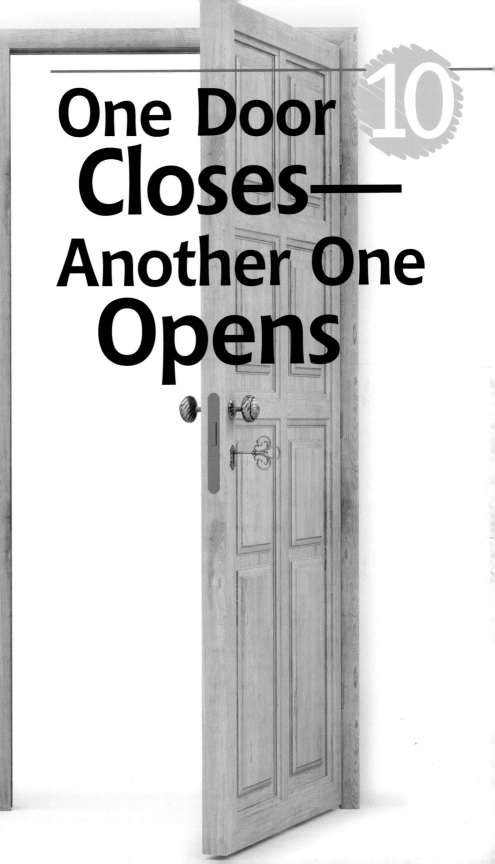

# One Door Closes— Another One Opens

10

# The Greed Factor

Before you grow your business into a success, define what success will look like for you. If it involves a certain level of value in your company and you reach that target, don't let greed force you to hold out for more. That could backfire and leave you with little or nothing.

Things are going really well in your company. You're generating revenue, you have a good network, some intellectual property, long-term contracts and even an interested buyer. This is a critical time in your career, and it is so important that you avoid something to which we are all susceptible: the greed factor. Many people fall into the trap of thinking that if one person is interested in buying their company, there is probably someone else out there willing to pay more. Let me tell you, the grass is not always greener on the other side.

Four times I was in a position to sell my first company, and four times I was unable to make the deal. My board of directors wanted to hold out for more. "Push back for another $3 million!" they said. "Get more cash up front instead of over time!" they insisted. "We are worth more. We can get more!" they repeated.

"They" were people with an important role in my business and, rightfully, had a major say in whether or not I could sell it. They had invested a lot of money in the company and, understandably, wanted to ensure that they would get a fair return. But what is a fair return? That is the question, and the answer depends on who is answering it and how they are looking at it. To me, a fair return was ensuring that I had enough money to take care of my family now and in the future.

I had started my company with a vision. I had updated that vision over the years to meet changing circumstances, but I always knew exactly what I was trying to accomplish. My firm goal from the outset, which I told everyone who invested with me, was that I was building the company to sell it. As soon as I got someone interested in giving me $1 million, I would take it. The challenge, because I had many shareholders, was that, even though I wanted $1 million, in order to get that sum I would have to sell the company at a multiple of $1 million so that everyone could get a return on their investment. If I could get $10 million or $100 million, for sure I would take it, but my goal was not going to waver from that $1 million. If I could reach it within a couple of years, I would take it without a second thought. I had seen deals go south, people change their minds and companies that were thought to be worth much more drop in value when the market changed. I wasn't about to take the risk of thinking I could get more and then, if something happened, lose everything.

When people heard that I was willing to take $1 million as soon as I could, their reaction was always the same: a million dollars is not a lot of money, and if you are doing well, why not go for more? Well, first of all, $1 million is a ton of money. To put it into perspective, consider the average salary, which is about $40,000 per year. At that income level, it would take a person 25 years to bring home $1 million. Now let's put it into a more realistic perspective. Once you remove taxes, car payments, mortgage, food, gas, heat, hydro and all the other bills associated with day-to-day living, you are left with almost nothing. In almost all cases like this, a person will never in their entire life be able to save $1 million.

## Establish what your walk-away goal is and stick to it. Don't be greedy or you might lose more than you think.

Another reason why I wouldn't try to get more had to do with the valuation of the company. I said my base price was $1 million, but if I could get more I would definitely go after it, especially if I thought my company was worth more. But valuation is really dependent on what a purchaser is willing to pay, especially when you are talking about a company that is still young and growing. You can, if you wish, set a much higher valuation based on trends in your sales, even though you do not have the sales to justify a high valuation right now.

And this is where the greed factor plays a role. You think that your company is going to have great sales, but there is still no guarantee that it will. As prospective buyers see it, they are being asked to pay you for value that is not yet realized and may never be realized. They want to pay less and you want them to pay more. If both sides cannot agree, the deal dies and you might never get another offer again. The market conditions might change, competitors might begin to dominate your market, and so forth. There are so many ways that something can go wrong and prevent you from ever selling.

In the end, each of the four possible chances I had to sell my company fell through because of the greed factor. The prospective buyers all told me my company was not worth what I thought it was, and they were right. Four great opportunities slipped through my hands because my stakeholders wanted to hold out for more. My goals were pushed aside in the attempt to get more money for my company. I do believe that, if we had structured the deal properly, we could all have benefited, but the decision was, unfortunately, not only up to me.

One of these four missed opportunities was particularly frustrating. I had built up a relationship with CSS, one of Hallmark's competitors out of the United States. I had met many times with their CEO and had started to build a relationship. We discussed what my company had to offer and how we might be able to advance their licensing opportunities not only in Canada, but abroad as well. In time, we began to talk about a possible acquisition, and in discussing an acquisition strategy the subject of valuation arose. This was my first introduction to an "earn-out" acquisition deal. By such a deal, CSS would acquire my company based on what they thought it was worth and commit to paying us additional funds in the future based on future financial successes. Despite my efforts to convince the board that this was a good deal, in the end the decision was made not to proceed with it. The board felt we could get more if we only waited and kept increasing our sales. Of course, that didn't happen. Other events intervened and changed everything.

Another important lesson learned: if your goal when you start out is to sell your company, come up with a dollar amount that you would be satisfied with taking, and set up your company so that you cannot be prevented from selling it when the time is right for you. If you get an offer that comes anywhere near your dollar goal, take it. Don't let greed interfere with the decision.

# The Toughest Decision

The decision, under very trying circumstances, to shut down the business you have worked so long and hard to build, is one you never want to think you'll have to make. But as it is with all difficult decisions, when your back is against the wall, you have to make the call, learn from the experience and move on.

I never did sell my first company. I was forced to close it due to the last recession. The market went into near economic meltdown in 2008, and the chance of getting other offers to buy my company went out the door. Sales declined, some of our customers were going bankrupt and buyers suddenly had much tighter budgets.

But we did make one more attempt to sell the business. At the request of my board, I went back to CSS—the company that, earlier, had offered us an earn-out deal—to try to reopen the door for an acquisition. I knew this was unlikely because the crash had affected everyone and they would be experiencing their own challenges. And, indeed, I was correct: they were no longer interested in entertaining opportunities with our company.

Just as these disastrous events were unfolding, we experienced another big blow. Paul, one of our board members and a very good friend, died unexpectedly. Paul was a well-respected and hard-working supporter of the business. His surprising death, coming as it did on top of the other heavy blows, made the challenges we were facing even greater.

As a board, we had to look at the chances of our company recovering, keeping in mind the loss of sales, the level of effort that would be required and the amount of money we would have to come up with to cover obligations that were coming due. In the end, we made the decision to wind down the company. This was an extremely difficult decision. I had worked hard to build this business and sacrificed almost everything I had for close to a decade. It is surprising how quickly things can change. Only two years earlier, sales were on the rise, business was expanding globally, new investments were coming in and we were buying out shareholders at twice their original investment. The company had employed many people, including me, who would now be out of work. It had half the number of shareholders, which still included me, who would also now lose their investment. Our suppliers, too, would suffer by losing our business. Having to close a company I had built from nothing but an idea to a multimillion-dollar operation was, to say the least, a very emotional decision. I had been used to making hard decisions—it goes with the territory. But this was the hardest of them all.

Not one to dwell on the negative, I took this difficult experience as another important lesson learned. I had no choice. My wife was a stay-at-home mother, we had three children now, a significant mortgage, bills starting to pile up, and I needed to *keep moving forward*. This is a phrase I keep in mind even to this day to remind myself that we *always* need to be looking ahead. I would move on and not make the same mistakes again.

# Once an Entrepreneur...

A true entrepreneur doesn't just give up and go away if one business venture doesn't work out. With the many experiences, good and bad, you have had with the previous company, you are well equipped to start a new one and turn it into a success—this time, success as defined by you.

Once an entrepreneur, always an entrepreneur! After the closure of my company, I did some consulting work for about a year and ended up returning to work with Scott Hunter, this time as the Project Management Centre's vice-president of training. This provided me with a base salary that would help cover my personal obligations, but that didn't last long. Having been self-employed for so long and used to giving directions and being in charge of my own opportunities, I did not want to be an employee, so I decided that I would again go out on my own. I wanted to start a second business.

## Being in charge of my own fate is what drives me as an entrepreneur. What drives you?

In the eight years between my leaving PMC and returning, the relationship between Scott and me had evolved from one of employer-employee to peer-peer. It only seemed natural, then, that we would become business partners. He had followed my ups and downs with my first company and had always expressed confidence in me, and that meant a lot to me. So he and I came up with an idea for a new business, outside PMC, and we worked up a deal in which we would be 50/50 partners. I would build the company and Scott would be my support, both from a financial and a strategic perspective. This was done by leveraging the financial strength of his company, PMC.

iPal Interactive Learning was born, and the arrangement Scott and I had, with him as CEO and me as president, worked perfectly as neither of us cared about the titles. It was about trust, confidence and communication. Scott was a great business partner, providing me with a sounding board for my ideas and strategies as well as the freedom, resources and confidence I needed to move forward quickly. There were times, of course, when he would question the amount of money I was spending and get a little nervous about whether I was going down the right path. There was a point at which we had spent more than $440,000 off a loan we had received from the Business Development Bank of Canada and still had no sales. I could see why he would be a bit concerned, but I was not. I had planned it all out.

Just as with my first company, when I started out I had no industry experience in the field I was entering, no real credibility, no distribution and no sales. But I had experience in how to build a business, and plenty of it. I had learned from my first business that there are key elements—all the elements I have talked about in this book—that you need to have working together in order to build a successful business. Many of these elements have to be put in place before you launch the company. During the development of iPal, I faced many of the same start-up challenges I had encountered with EasyWrapLines. I approached them the same way I had before, brainstorming what I wanted to do and where I wanted the business to be in five years. Next, I looked at what I needed to do to build the business, jotting down all ideas, no matter how trivial they seemed. Based on these, I drew up a plan outlining the steps that would be required in order to move forward on all fronts: sales, marketing, developing credibility, creating products, getting resources, and so on.

Once all the planning was completed and we were ready to launch the product into the market, Scott's concerns were soon put aside. Success came much more quickly with this new venture than it had with my first company. Within the first five months after launch, we had landed several clients in a variety of industries and sales were trending towards $1 million. Learning from my previous business experience, the good and the bad, I was able to build this second company with a greater diversity of clients and substantially more company value. There were two key reasons for this: I knew what I was doing, and I had strong and immediate support from my business partner. With solid financial resources behind me, I was able to hire a team right from the start to help achieve our goal. Because of my previous experience, I was able to avoid many of the pitfalls I had encountered before, staying away from potential threats and marketing the company with both revenue and value in mind. Less than 18 months after we started the company, we were in a position to sell it.

# A Successful Sale

The successful sale of a company involves getting what you think is a fair deal for both you and the buyer. For yourself, this means getting the target amount you set at the beginning—and, if possible, more. It does not mean repeatedly holding out for more and more and running the risk of getting less, or nothing.

There were several reasons I was upset and disappointed when we had to close my first company. One of them, of course, was the fact that I had not been able to sell the business and get the $1 million I had set as my target at the beginning. I was determined not to make the same mistakes again. I would set up my new company so that, when the time came to exit, I could make the decision based on my personal objectives. And that is exactly what I did.

When I built iPal, I set it up so that we would sell it for a minimum of $1 million, with the understanding that we would get as much as we reasonably could over that amount. But we would not make the mistake of always thinking that holding out for more would necessarily bring us more. My business partner, Scott, agreed to sign documents to this effect. We also included a clause that would prevent any future investors from having any control over our exit strategy. Only 18 months after launching the company into the market, we were in a position to work out an acquisition.

The acquisition began from a conversation I had with the CEO of the interested company. We were asking him to sign a letter demonstrating that they were indeed one of our customers and that we had an agreement to develop a certain number of courses for him. While discussing this, I mentioned that we needed this letter as part of our due diligence for potential investors. One thing led to the next, and the CEO indicated interest in possibly becoming an investor. At first, it seemed like a suggestion, but not a serious one. However, he had opened the door and I was curious now—might they be interested in more than an investment? An acquisition, perhaps? Knowing that this company had purchased several other companies, I thought that if I positioned the opportunity to him in a fair manner, one that would be a win-win for both parties, my chances of a sale were good.

At this time, iPal was trending towards the million-dollar mark in revenue. Many organizations now considered iPal an industry leader and were looking to adopt our methodology for their training programs. I was being invited to speak at important conferences in the areas of health and education. Scott and I felt that, with the value we had built in the company, we could probably get a multiple that could be in the millions of dollars. The trick was to appraise the company at a fair value so that potential acquirer would see that we were not being greedy, while also ensuring that we could get as much as we possibly could. Over the course of the next few weeks, the CEO and I talked again, and when I went to his office to discuss how he might become a shareholder, I also came prepared with a plan to make this company our purchaser, should they be interested. When I pulled out the paper with the details of my plan, he was a bit surprised ("Wow, you don't waste any time!"), but he also expressed interest. I hadn't messed around trying to come up with a purchase price, because I figured he wouldn't see the future value of the company right away. The important thing was that we arrive at what we both saw as a win-win deal.

# If you make the deal a win-win, both parties will feel valued

One of the things that drew me to this company in the first place was the fact that they were not all about the money. People were important to them. Before the CEO made a decision about acquiring a company, he and his team would meet the key people on the other team to see what they were like and if the two groups seemed to be a comfortable fit. In the course of that process, he asked me a rather interesting question: How many people in the company were being paid more that I was? I told him that, at the time, there were three: the programmer, design manager and design lead. "It could be better for me personally, but I needed to make sure my staff were paid first." He agreed and smiled. He said he thought that showed good leadership—thinking about the success of your business before your own. We were on the same page, and the acquisition was completed.

In the end, Scott and I got exactly what we wanted and the company got a great deal on the business and an opportunity to build an even larger one with me involved. We were not greedy. We provided a fair opportunity for both parties, and worked out an arrangement that provided us with the financial payment I was seeking as well as the opportunity for much more in the future. The deal was perfect! It is important to note that a deal is only as successful as the continuing efforts made after closing.

• • • • •

With the sale of iPal, I agreed to stay on with the company for a period of time. With growth and change come new roles, and learning doesn't stop. When I moved into this corporate environment as part of their executive team, it was great to see that entrepreneurship was encouraged. But the challenge for me was that this new culture was not as entrepreneurial as the one I had become accustomed to. I learned quickly that the executives at the new company were all brilliant, well-educated, experienced professionals in their field and, most important, they embraced continual learning. Although entrepreneurship was encouraged, most people within the corporation were not entrepreneurs.

Being part of a human resources firm meant embracing personal and professional development. The transition would be difficult for me and, being an entrepreneur through and through, the CEO understood this well. He understood that iPal, under his company, would start to grow quickly, which would also create an environment of continual change, employee stress and employee growth. Additional management would be required. He indicated that he had previously experienced this type of growth within a young, high-growth company, so he decided to meet with me to discuss how we could best handle what was to come. His combined experiences as an entrepreneur as well as a corporate man allowed him to see that I would need support to help curb my entrepreneurial zeal and start operating at a corporate level. The solution he felt was a personal executive coach. Instead of trying to change the way I was, he wanted to help me grow and build on what I had already learned. I embraced this opportunity because I knew that, with the growth iPal was about to face, I would need to set up a middle management team and hire dozens of new staff, and to do these things well, I would have to start thinking differently. I would not be losing my entrepreneurial style and thinking, but now I could start to gain knowledge from others on how to build and manage more effectively than I had done previously.

Being open to advice at all levels helps you become a better entrepreneur, employee, manager and even leader. The day we stop listening to what others have to say is the day we think we know everything—and the day we start to fail ourselves and the people around us.

**Being part of a new environment meant that change would be required, but it could not be one-sided. Both sides would have to learn to adapt in order to be supportive and successful.**

As a child I was introverted and insecure, with a serious learning disability. It was so bad that during my elementary school years, at the ripe old age of 10, my special education teacher told me I should not get my hopes up for a scholarly career but should aim for something like construction work. When I was 13, the highlight of my Christmas Eve was finding a bunch of broken toys as I rummaged around with my brothers in the bottom of a dumpster.

Today, however, I am outgoing, successful, financially well off and happy. In hindsight, I am convinced that my difficult childhood was an advantage—it made me the entrepreneur I am today. I had to teach myself at a young age how to resolve issues, solve problems and look for creative solutions. I learned to react quickly, seeing opportunity where others saw none and solutions where others saw only problems. I learned to turn nothing into something, and to turn that something into something more.

When you grow up struggling to survive, the problems you encounter—no matter how big or small—will eventually seem like they're not a big deal. It's like watching scary movies. The more you watch, the more desensitized you become and the less scary they seem. I faced difficult challenges at a very young age, and that became part of my learning experiences, a part of me. I had to learn to adapt in order to survive.

# 11

# A Glance Back

I AM OFTEN ASKED WHETHER I WOULD GO BACK IN time and change my difficult childhood, if I could. As a child, I would have said yes in an instant. But now I understand the value of my experiences, and if I had the option, I would keep everything exactly as it was. Experience is the best educator anyone can have. My education included a tough childhood, a constant fear of failure, a struggle for survival and the intense desire to be greater than I was. Through it all, I learned that no matter how bad things might get, tomorrow would always bring a new, and maybe even more exciting, adventure.

Over the years, I have used all the elements of my challenging childhood—in adapted versions, of course—to help me climb out of the dumpster, get a decent job and fulfill my entrepreneurial dreams by growing a multimillion-dollar business. I have been published in *The Globe and Mail*, the *PMI Networker*, and the newsletters of both the Canadian and American Societies for Training and Development (CSTD and ASTD), on theories and solutions to industry problems. I have been a member of many well-respected boards and have been president of the Project Management Institute's Ottawa chapter. I have travelled the world several times, I vacation every year with my family and I own a beautiful home with a pool oasis in my own backyard. Most important, I am happily married, the father of three fantastic kids and am able to provide for my family in a way that I could only dream about when I was that scared, struggling teenager. Finally, I am happy. People have asked me over the years how I would define success. It is being happy. If you are happy, that probably also means that you have a balance between your personal and business lives.

My success did not happen overnight. Rather, it was the result of many years of sacrifice, hard work and building credibility. My struggles came with tears, pain, fear, regret and embarrassment, but through them all I kept moving forward and survived. Through this book, I hope I have shown how you too can find your strength when you feel weak, can stay passionate when others tell you to give up, can be persistent when doors are closing and, above all, succeed without sacrificing what is most important in your life.

# Keep Moving Forward

When building a company, it is always important to keep moving forward. When you stand still, others around you are marching ahead, which means you will start to fall behind. Keep moving forward!

When I look back at what I have been able to accomplish, the main lesson I have learned about becoming a successful entrepreneur is not that you have to be smarter or work harder; it is that you must never give up. You will try and try and try right until the end. You will keep moving forward, regardless of the failures you have encountered. Success or failure is only the consequence of trying. The fact that you continue to try is what makes you an entrepreneur. Being successful will not happen right away. If it does happen quickly, count yourself blessed. For the majority of us, including me, it took a long time. You have to work hard, long hours, experience failure, endure criticism and, in the end, you need to pick yourself back up time and time again. *Always keep moving forward!* If you can do that, you will eventually succeed.

When the going was hard, I would tell myself I had to go on if I wanted to change my life. I would try to think beyond my short-term goals, but look ahead, thinking of new ideas, new innovations and ways to stay ahead of my competitors. I would focus not only on today, but also on tomorrow and the days after that. A vision can only come true if you are moving towards the future.

Even now, I am focused on building iPal Interactive Learning into a global leader in e-learning. I am focused, with my growing team, on international partnerships, establishing global credibility, opening up new channels of distribution for education and creating more future value back to the company that acquired us. I have also established monthly innovation meetings with my creative teams to ensure that they too are always thinking ahead so that we can lead the market. I am working to generate "thought leaders" within iPal so that the market can learn from our experiences. This requires the development of articles, white papers or lectures through which people on my team will transfer their knowledge to the industry. This will help to ensure that we are again being seen as leaders and drive more credibility our way. It is this credibility that will continue to attract more people to our website and our services and help continue to expand our opportunities. As I continue to gain more sales, I am still focused on the fundamentals of what I have learned over the years, and I still follow the examples I have laid out in this book.

With more opportunities come more complications, and so long as I stay the course, practise what I preach and keep moving forward, more success will continue to come my way and to the company I have built.

# Entrepreneurship to Leadership

As mentioned earlier, I am working with an executive coach to help me think beyond entrepreneurship and to help me work to move into more of a leadership role. Building a multimillion-dollar company is one thing, but when your vision involves the building of a multi*billion*-dollar company, that is another level of management all together. I understand that if I want to build bigger and better, I need to rely more on my team to transform my vision into reality. I cannot continue to dive into the weeds with the designers to come up with a better graphic. I need to focus on instilling my values and hiring around the behaviours that will help drive the business towards this success.

I have always been an entrepreneur and always will be. However, just as I had to learn to adapt to a changing entrepreneurial environment, so too I found that I had to learn to adapt to success. Moving into a leadership role was a new experience for me. Even though I was good at most positions I took on, being a leader required me to take a step back and move my thinking from doing to leading.

In understanding how to become a better leader, the CEO of the new company felt I needed to be assessed in order to determine the type of leader I was. This is a standard practice with all executives whom they employed. This assessment, known as the Birkman Method, combines hundreds of questions together to assess the motivational and behavioural characteristics and interests of a leader. The results of this assessment, through a combination of regression and factor analysis, would help identify my everyday interpersonal style, give insights into my underlying motivations and needs. My stress behaviours when my needs are not met would also be identified. Understanding the underlying motivations and the consequences of these unmet needs would help provide my employer and my personal executive coach with a more effective understanding of who I am and how I behave under stress and other conditions.

I was extremely nervous about taking this assessment. Having been assessed before as a child, I felt anxious and apprehensive right away. I was concerned that I would fail, and even though you can't fail an assessment, I knew I would be judged, and I wasn't up for that. I was interested, however, in improving and growing as a leader, and I knew this was part of that process. There were many people from Head Office who were also anxious to see the results of my assessment. I had a feeling that there were some who were also more interested in seeing the report as proof of my inadequacies. Nevertheless, I was doing this assessment for myself and for how it could help me improve.

## Do things for yourself and not for others. You are your own judge of your life.

Once I completed the assessment, a conference call was set up with a Birkman expert, my coach and a person from human resources at Head Office. Leading up to this day, I was told several times about how the information I was going to receive was confidential and that I was going to hear things that might make me feel uncomfortable, revelations that would reflect who I was as a leader. They wanted to ensure that I was in a room where no one could hear me, that my phone should not be on speaker and that I needed to be prepared. I had received the results of the assessment a week before the consultation and had been told that

I should not read the results of the assessment until everyone was together so that I could truly understand. I stayed true to this and did not review it. I was so busy that, to be honest, I would not have had the time anyway.

The day finally came. An hour-and-a-half time slot set aside to talk about why I do what I do while industry experts walked through what makes me tick.

## Being an entrepreneur usually means that you are not like other people. That is okay!

When the Birkman expert first started to speak, she started off by saying that after reviewing my assessment, she was surprised, shocked and uncertain about some of the results. She mentioned that what she had read and what she was going to explain to me was unique, that it was unlike almost every assessment she had seen. She went on to say I was a rare person and that this assessment was something she had never seen before.

As we moved through the assessment, page after page, the Birkman expert continued to point out that I was definitely an entrepreneur, and the results showed that. She repeated that I was rare and that she was so impressed with the results. I replied that I guessed that meant I got another A. The results showed positive balances across the board. Everyone on the conference call was surprised and commented on how unusual it was to have results like these. The assessment was designed to give insights into someone's true nature, and with me, there were elements that were inexplicable. For example, the expert asked us to turn to a page about stress; the page was blank. The women on the call asked how this was possible, and the expert replied that she did not know. She observed that everyone has stress and that this page was meant to show what stress factors I needed to manage. She asked me if I had an explanation for the result, and I did. I told her my upbringing had not been easy. There were many stress factors that had threatened my core survival. This had continued for many years, and it was because of this that I became use to dealing with stress. It wasn't that I did not have any stress, but rather that I was able to manage it. It takes a lot to get me stressed out because I have been through a lot. After this explanation, they all agreed that it made the most sense.

The positive reviews and comments continued. There were, of course, elements that tied into understanding how I deal with different types of situations and people, but even those were quite positive.

The last review was probably the most telling as far as my entrepreneurial nature was concerned. It was a chart that mapped my understanding, skills, abilities and interests across all levels of an organization. This chart showed the level of intensity I would bring to these areas and help outline my areas of strength as well as those I might need to work on improving.

What was surprising to everyone on the call, including myself, was the intensity of the bands across each of the levels. It was interesting to hear the HR person from Head Office ask how this was possible. According to my assessment results, the intensity of the bands was fairly consistent across all streams. The reason behind this is entrepreneurship. As an entrepreneur I had been forced to learn, adapt and become good at all areas because I didn't have the resources to hire around them. Developing plans, selling, creating marketing materials, managing financials, setting up production and overseeing infrastructure all support what it means to be an entrepreneur and build a business. These results demonstrated that I could be dropped into any one of these streams and be able to manage it effectively—which is not to say I would enjoy each stream, just that I have levels of interest within each.

# Tomorrow Will Always Come

No matter what has gone wrong today, tomorrow always comes. The world moves forward and we, as entrepreneurs, have to learn how to adapt to our changing environment. Even as I was writing this book, there were many changes and challenges that I was faced with and had to deal with. Some of the challenges are difficult ones, and I am staying focused to get through them. All it requires is that we *Keep moving forward!*

Brad is a serial entrepreneur. He is a natural innovator, problem-solver, visionary, leader and people person. He brings several decades of leadership and hands-on management experience in the industries of project management, entertainment, design and online education. He has held many positions over the years including garbage picker, dishwasher, cook, waiter, chamber "maid", pizza delivery boy, construction worker, grocery cashier, retail clerk, forklift driver and call centre representative. Focusing on improving his life, by 2001 Brad had received his designation as a Project Management Professional (PMP) from the Project Management Institute and from there grew his career by leveraging this discipline into his entrepreneurial nature. Over the years that followed, Brad became a part-time project management professor at Algonquin College, a program manager with the Bank of Canada and the Vice-President of Training with PMC. Brad eventually worked his way onto the Board of Directors with PMI-OVOC where he supported the Communication and Public Relation portfolio and completed his term three years later as the chapter's youngest president.

Through his PM discipline and professional experiences, Brad founded several companies that reached over a million dollars in revenue within a few years of inception and has grown to become more than a one-off successful entrepreneur. He continues to build more business today as he travels the world establishing relationships and partnerships, and fostering opportunities to help facilitate his vision of providing top education to anyone, anywhere, anytime.

Throughout his professional career, Brad has been awarded Ottawa's Top 40 Under 40 Entrepreneurial Award and a Bronze Award for Small Business of the Year presented by the Ottawa Chamber of Commerce. He has also been recognized for his thought leadership being published in *The Globe and Mail*, *PM Network*, and Canadian Society of Training and Development (CSTD) and American Society of Training and Development (ASTD) publications. Brad is a passionate and outspoken entrepreneur who has been featured on CBC Venture, CTV News, CJOH, CBC News and in many local and national newspapers. He has spoken at many leadership conferences such as the CSTD, the Aboriginal Entrepreneurship Conference, the Mental Health Conference, the Cultural Human Resources Conference and the Service Canada Instructional Design Conference.

Brad is a true believer that success comes to those who focus on the relationships and a mutually beneficial outcome. It must be a win-win in order to be a success.